W9-BVQ-173

SHELTON STATE COMMUNITY
COLLEGE
JUNIOR COLLEGE DIVISION
LIBRARY

DISCARDED

BR   Belloc, Hilaire, 1870–1953.
115
.C5   The crisis of civilization.
B33
1973

DATE DUE

DEC 0 5 1990			
DEC 0 5 1990			
DEC 0 5 1990			

THE CRISIS
OF
CIVILIZATION

THE CRISIS

of

CIVILIZATION

HILAIRE BELLOC

GREENWOOD PRESS, PUBLISHERS
WESTPORT, CONNECTICUT

The Library of Congress has catalogued this publication as follows:

Library of Congress Cataloging in Publication Data

Belloc, Hilaire, 1870-1953.
  The crisis of civilization.

  CONTENTS: The foundation of Christendom.--Christendom
established.--The Reformation and its immediate consequences. [etc.]
  1. Civilization, Christian. 2. Sociology, Christian
(Catholic) I. Title.
BR115.C5B33 1973   261.8'3   73-114465
ISBN 0-8371-4761-1

Originally published in 1937 by Fordham University
Press, New York

Reprinted in 1973 by Greenwood Press,
a division of Congressional Information Service,
88 Post Road West, Westport, Connecticut 06881

Library of Congress catalog card number 73-114465

ISBN 0-8371-4761-1

Printed in the United States of America

10 9 8 7 6 5 4 3 2

THE CRISIS OF CIVILIZATION

*Being the matter of a
Course of Lectures
delivered at Fordham
University 1937*

INTRODUCTION

THIS WORK CONTAINS the matter of the lectures I delivered at Fordham University between the 16th February and the 18th May, 1937. To put the matter in book form I have arranged it not by single lectures but by groups into which my thesis naturally falls. That thesis may be discovered in the title I have given to the whole, *The Crisis of Civilization.* It is an historical presentation to the following effect:

That our civilization, that is, the civilization of Christendom, today occupying Europe, especially Western Europe, and radiating thence over the New World, acting also as a leader or instructor of the other cultures in Asia and Northern Africa, has arrived at a crisis where it is in peril of death. I propose therefore to describe how that civilization arose, upon what main lines it developed, what institutions it produced and depended upon, and when it was at its height. I next propose to show historically how it became disunited and thereby spiritually enfeebled while materially progressing, until at last with the destruction of the moral tradition by which it had existed and was precariously maintained, even while that tradition was weakening, it lost its very principle of life and may therefore, unless we return to that principle, dissolve.

My thesis in other words is this:

That the culture and civilization of Christendom—what was called for centuries in general terms "Europe," was made by the Catholic Church gathering up the social traditions of the Graeco-Roman Empire, inspiring them and giving the whole of that great body a new life. It was the Catholic Church which made us, gave us our unity and our

1

whole philosophy of life, and formed the nature of the white world. That world—Christendom—went through the peril of the barbaric assault from without as also from the victorious pressure of great heresy—which soon became a new religion—Mahommedanism.

These perils it survived, though shorn of much of its territory; it re-arose after the pressure was past to the high life of the Middle Ages, which in the 11th, 12th, and especially the 13th centuries reached a climax or summit wherein we were most ourselves and our civilization most assured. But from various causes of which perhaps old age was the chief, that great period showed signs of decline at the beginning of the 14th century; a decline which hastened rapidly throughout the 15th century. The Faith by which we live was increasingly doubted; and the moral authority upon which all depended was more and more contested. The society of Christendom underwent a heavy strain threatening disruption; it equally became more and more unstable, until at last in the early 16th century came the explosion which had been feared and awaited for so long. That disaster is called in general usage "The Reformation."

From that moment onwards throughout the 16th and 17th centuries and the 18th, on through the 19th, the unity of Christendom having disappeared and the vital principle on which its life depended having become weak or distracted, our culture became a house divided against itself, and increasingly imperiled. This evil fortune was accompanied by a rapid increase in external knowledge, that is in science and the command of man over material things, even as he lost his grasp of spiritual truths. It was the converse of what had happened in the beginning of our civilization, when our religion had saved the ancient world and formed a new culture, though burdened by a decline in science and the arts and material things.

Our increase in knowledge of the externals and in our power over nature did nothing to appease the rapidly growing internal strains of our world. The conflict between rich and poor, the conflict between opposing national idolatries, the lack of common standards and of the fixed doctrines upon which they depend had led up by the beginning of the 20th century to the brink of chaos; and threatened such dissention between men as to destroy Society. In this crisis the only alternatives are recovery through the restoration of Catholicism or the extinction of our culture.

Such is the scheme of the series of addresses delivered, and of this book in which the matter of them is put before the reader. I have divided it not according to single lectures but according to certain groups, five in number, to which the progress of those addresses corresponded.

The first group deals with the *Foundation of Christendom* by the conversion of the Græco-Roman Empire just before it failed from despair, but not in time to save it from material decline. That process covers roughly the first five centuries of our era.

The next group deals with the great ordeal wherein civilization was tested and with difficulty emerged—what I have called the *The Siege of Christendom,* whence arose the corresponding high moment of the True Middle Ages, to be followed by their decline. It is a period of roughly a thousand years, from the 6th to the 15th century inclusive. It falls naturally into three subdivisions: the Siege of Christendom, the High Middle Ages and their Decline.

The third group concerns the *Reformation,* that is the disruption of our society, and the sowing of those seeds which were later to threaten our very existence; the independence of each separate province of Christendom from the rest, the denial of any common moral authority over them, the affirmation of the Sovereign State owing allegiance to none and free to destroy any of its fellows, and open itself to a similar fate without appeal; the destruction of coöperative social life and the growing tyranny of wealth.

The fourth group is concerned with the process whereby these moral and social evils following on the disruption of Christendom, coupled with a rapidly increasing knowledge of nature and a consequent development of communications and all external aptitudes, led at last to the opposition throughout what had once been the Christian world, of the rich against the poor; the partial enslavement of the latter, their destitution, their dependence upon a minority of pay-masters—the reaction against such inhuman conditions of insufficiency and insecurity and the formulating of this reaction first in the vague terms of what used to be called *Socialism,* later the precise, doctrinal and intense form of what is now universally known as *Communism.* Communism and its opponent, the Catholic Church, the traditions by which Christendom had been formed and lived and the proposal to destroy those traditions altogether, particularly the religion upon which everything depends, now stand face to face.

The fifth group concerns the *suggested remedies* for a situation so desperate; for if Communism be accepted as an apparent solution it is the end of our culture, of all by which we have lived.

There only remains as an alternative to apply the fruits which the Catholic culture had produced when it was in full vigor, the restriction of monopoly, the curbing of the money power, the establishment of coöperative work, and the wide distribution of private property, the main principle of the guild and the jealous restriction of usury and competition, which between them have come so near to destroying us. But these better conditions are themselves the fruits of the Catholic Church, they can neither be created nor maintained in an atmosphere deprived of Catholic philosophy. The conclusion of the series is therefore that in the reconversion of our world to the Catholic standpoint lies the only hope for the future.

I

THE FOUNDATION OF CHRISTENDOM

I would lay it down at the beginning that the present crisis in our civilization is the gravest affecting that civilization since first it took on its essential character, between 1900 and 1600 years ago.

During the whole of that very long period of time there has been present upon this earth and in that district of the world which seems to have been set apart for the leadership thereof a well-defined recognizable culture, to which our forefathers gave the appropriate name—Christendom. It arose upon a certain foundation, the pagan Græco-Roman Empire of antiquity; it developed through the impact and influence upon this of the Catholic Church; it grew in spiritual character and energy throughout some 500 years in the midst of which Catholicism had already become the accepted philosophy, morals and religion of our blood. It even expanded beyond the boundaries of that highly civilized antique state wherein it arose, it transformed the heathen beyond the boundaries of that state, spreading to include outer parts of it which the original Roman policy had not directly ruled; it suffered attack from without and grave material decline from within, but it survived.

It not only survived but flowered after a long ordeal during the Dark Ages, and was perhaps at its highest in the centuries immediately following, the 11th, 12th, 13th, 14th, and 15th, which we call the Middle Ages. Having so expanded, withstood its first perils and grown established, it suffered 400 years ago a peril of disruption. It was nearly destroyed by internal faction; dispute upon its primary and creative doctrines wrecked in part at least its main institutions. But so much of it yet again survived as to maintain the continuity of culture. Christendom, though at war within itself during the 16th and 17th centuries was still Christendom; the primary doctrines and their consequent social habits (whereby Europe and her expansion overseas lived) still stood in the general mind of men. But the struggle had been heavy, the loss of unity and therefore of personality in that great body was increasingly apparent.

At first a minority only lost the full Christian traditions and till the late 18th century the mass of Europe itself and the colonies which Europe had planted beyond the ocean, still lived by the rules, if not of Faith, at any rate, of accepted conduct which they had inherited from so great a past.

But the process of dissolution continued. During the 19th century the core of the affair was diluted and grew weaker; certain prime established things which had formed the structure of Christendom were shaken. Within two generations they were tottering. The characteristic unity of Christendom was already more than half forgotten; each of its parts, now wholly separate, had already long arrogated to itself complete sovereignty, and therefore implicitly denied the corporate life of the whole; while within the structure institutions which were bound

7

into the common heritage, cementing it and giving it unity, were dissolving.

Marriage was beginning to be challenged, therefore the family; property still stood, but its moral basis was questioned. Civil authority had gone the way of spiritual, its basis was disputed and its security failing. The ancient canon of morals, the chief characteristic of Christendom, in sexual and personal as in general and civil relations, was challenged, doubted and confused. It was losing its vigor, changing from an unquestioned fixity to a debated mass of fluid opinion. All this process reached its climax in our own time.

Meanwhile there has necessarily proceeded side by side with the general decay of the ancient and once apparently permanent moral structure, a social and economic change springing from the same roots but of more immediate consequence, because it directly affects the lives of men in a fashion that each can appreciate and with which all were directly and vividly concerned.

The livelihood of men had become insecure; over wide departments of many nations in the most part of Society there had arisen insecurity and destitution on such a scale that life threatened to be soon intolerable for its victims. Even as this awful challenge to human life approached its climax, all hope of dealing with it by a commonly accepted philosophy seemed to have been lost.

In other words, that by which the leaders of mankind had lived, that by which the white civilization had been what it was, that from which what had been for so long most properly called Christendom, had drawn its personality, its will, its honor, its very self, was and is melting away.

It is with justice then that we speak of the *Crisis of Our Civilization*. It is with justice that we apply that very grave term to the moment in which we have the misfortune or the combative glory to live.

So emphatic a description of the menace under which we lie may seem exaggerated to those who have not considered the contrast between today and the long centuries of accepted morals preceding it. It is not exaggerated. It is in due proportion and true. We are in peril here and now of losing all that by which and for which our fathers lived, and which we still know to be, though in apparently active dissolution, our inheritance.

In the presence of any great crisis the task in hand is the solution thereof; and as this crisis is the greatest of all historically known to us, the task before us is also the greatest and the arrival at a solution the most practical end which men of our blood have ever had set before them.

Throughout the world European and Transoceanic, uncertain efforts inspired by the necessity of arriving at some solution are beginning in a confused fashion. They differ in character, the two main schools in those who pursue these efforts are opposed and in mortal conflict— yet at some solution we must arrive and arrive in common. It is the business of this book to examine the nature of the problem and discover, if it be possible, the policy to be applied which may successfully dissipate the mortal threat overhanging us. The Sphinx has asked us its final and weightiest riddle, we must find an answer to it or die.

A crisis is of its nature a strain; it connotes unstable equilibrium. The settling of a crisis, the recovery of fixed and acceptable conditions, is the resolution of that strain. The strain arises from unstable equilibrium between the component parts and circumstances of anything: the unstable equilbrium must be reduced again to stability under pain of destruction. Thus in the nervous system of the human being there may arise a strain under which the faculties of intelligence and of will, the judgment of the senses, the whole balanced affair, falls into disarray. The strain will be resolved by the restoration of the coördinated faculties; that is, by the cure of the sufferer and his reëstablishment in sanity; or it will be resolved by a breakdown which we call madness, which is the death and end of sanity. A chemical combination when it is unstable must either be resolved by the separation of its component parts or the rearrangement of them in a stable form; or by letting the instability of them resolve itself in the disaster of an explosion, whereby that which was ceases to be.

Or take a building, a tall tower for example, which becomes unstable, leaning over at a perilous angle. We may pull it down in time and rebuild it or shore it up sufficiently to permit of strengthening its structure until it shall be fully established again; or we may act too late or unwisely, so that through our delay or blunder the mass will fall to the ground, cease to be what it was and be lost. Under any crisis (that is under any special strain), in order to act wisely and prevent the threatened disaster, we must discover two things: first, how serious it is, for only when we know that can we say whether this or that perhaps drastic and painful effort is worth while. Next, what are the causes at work which have produced the increasing tension.

Now in the case of the modern strain, in the case of this "final crisis of our civilization," wherein the quarrel between the dispossessed and the possessed, the exploited and the exploiter, the sufferer from injustice and the beneficiary therefrom threaten to pull down our world, there can be no question as to the seriousness of the issue. It is of maximum seriousness, it is as serious as it can be, and what is more it is immediate. It is upon us.

But as to its cause, that is another matter: it is because men dispute so much upon its cause that they differ so much as to the remedy. Yet unless we are right upon the cause and can choose the applicable remedy, we perish. Now how shall we make up our minds upon the cause, how shall we judge the inmost character of the thing with which we have to deal?

There is but one main method of approach, and that method is to follow and appreciate the history of the thing now in danger of death—our society. To understand how Christendom came to be and what is indeed the inmost principle whereby it was for so long that which it was, and only at this long last has come to sudden failure, we must follow its growth and maintenance. The problem is organic; we must appreciate the nature of the living thing in order to cure it, now that it is in mortal sickness. That nature we can only know by seeing how it was born, and grew, and lived.

What then was the story of Christendom, and why has that story now come to be threatened with an end? History upon all this is our guide; the history of what we were explains what we are.

Now in approaching any historical statement, especially upon approaching one concerned with a long historical process, and more particularly in approaching one of a wide scope such as this, there are certain rules to be observed; national and religious bias even more than the inevitable limitations of the individual student tend to warp the truth. But we can get as near an approximation of the truth as is reasonable to expect by keeping in mind certain postulates from which the rules of right historical judgment are to be drawn. Whether in the question I am now undertaking I have duly observed these rules it will be for those who read to judge; but I have attempted to observe them and I desire to state them thus at the outset, because they seem to me of the first importance. We are about to answer the main question, "What happened?" We are about to attempt the drawing of a large outline which shall be true: which corresponds to reality.

As it seems to me there are four main postulates in approaching any great social development historically.

The first postulate is this: *"Truth Lies in Proportion."* You do not tell an historical truth by merely stating a known fact; nor even by stating a number of facts in a certain and true order. You can tell it justly only by stating the known things in the order of their values.

It has been objected by unthinking men that history is necessarily uncertain because it necessarily consists in the facts selected by the narrator, and since he can leave out what he chooses the result may be almost anything. But this is to presuppose that the man who is telling the story is not desirous of presenting the truth. Suppose he be so desirous, he will only achieve his object by a just selection: that is by selection according to the order of value, giving chief weight to what is most important in connection with his narrative, less weight to what is less important, and omitting as he is bound to omit within any limits, however large, what is least important. This is especially clear in the case of general statement on so large a matter as the establishment of a civilization, its origin, character and development. But how and why it is proportion that determines history may be seen by a particular example.

Suppose a man who knows nothing of English literature say to you, "Who is William Shakespeare? I see his name continually; who and what was he?" If you answer, "He was a man of the middle class of society born near Stratford-on-Avon some three centuries and a half ago. He proceeded to London as a young man and there became an actor"—you are stating truths, but you are not stating *the* truth. You are not putting in your statement the main fact first. The true answer of course is, "William Shakespeare is the greatest writer of English, the greatest English poet, and among the very first poets of ancient and modern times." If your limits allow you to expand this statement you can next give his date, after that go into the nature of his work, then deal with his social position, with the amount of his known writing, and so forth. You could fill in the outline in as much detail as your space permits—but you must put the first things first and the second things second. If from ignorance or as is more probable from affection for this or that you give wrong values, emphasizing the lesser at the expense of the greater, you are not writing true history. You must of course in the process of your narration admit some word at least to show why such and such an element is more important than another; in other words, you must help to convince those whom you address of your good faith and competence; but anyhow, the main point is that historical truth lies (as does all judgment, that is a right appreciation of anything) upon a due grasp of proportion.

My second postulate will be less easily accepted than my first: it is that religion is the main determining element in the formation of a culture or civilization.

Some would use the word "philosophy" rather than religion. But a social philosophy, that is, an attitude with regard to the universe held by great numbers of men in common for long spaces of time and throughout a whole society, is inevitably and necessarily clothed with forms; it will always and necessarily have some liturgy of its own, some ritual, some symbols, even though it does not consciously affirm any transcendental doctrines. For example, the modern worship of the nation, the modern philosophy whereby our prime duty is regarded as being our duty to the State of which we are members—the general modern conception that affection for and loyalty towards our country is the chief political duty of man—is indeed a philosophy. But it is also in practice a religion, it has its symbols, its revered officers, its regular sequence of public ritual and all the rest of it. And if this is true of a mere philosophy, a mere mundane attitude towards visible and ephemeral things, it is quite certainly true of any positive strongly-held conviction upon the Divine element in the arrangements of mankind.

A group of human beings which believes, in general and firmly, that good or evil-doing in this life are followed by corresponding consequences after death, that the individual soul is immortal, that God is one and the common omnipotent Father of all, will behave in one way and a group which denies all reality in ideas of the sort will behave in another. A group which concentrates its spiritual vision upon the image of terrifying and even maleficent powers will behave thus and thus; another group which upon the whole contemplates more genial powers friendly to man and in tune with beauty will act otherwise. The whole of a human group is given its savor and character by the spirit which thus inhabits it; and that spirit may justly be called in nearly every case a religion—although if the term be preferred it may (in cases where the sense of mystery is weak) be termed a philosophy.

But whatever name they give it, on that religion or philosophy, the character of those who hold it in common will be founded as will the character of their philosophy or culture as a whole. If such and such things are held in awe, others in abhorrence, and others again presumed indifferent, such and such is the result upon Society as a whole. Change the elements, regard with abhorrence what was formerly thought of with indifference, with indifference what was formerly held sacred, and the whole character of your polity is transformed. This we can see today by comparing at least a part of the new world developing before our eyes with the work of the last generation: that older world the sanctions and sentiments of which so many are now abandoning.

Efforts have been made to give to some other element than this element of religion (or philosophy) the determining character in a civilization. Thus, many seek that determining character in race or blood: it is one of the most fashionable theories of the time in which we live. Others propose economic circumstances as the determining element and say that a polity is what it is through the way in which wealth is produced and distributed therein. But these and all other explanations are really no more than the restatement of a philosophy or religion. The man who makes race everything (as do many Germans today) is merely preaching a religion of race. The man who makes economic circumstance everything is merely preaching the religion of materialism. Indeed, to do them justice, both consciously proclaim this truth: that a culture is formed by its religion. The German Nazi enthusiast for Germanic excellence, one might almost say for Germanic divinity, proclaims his confidence therein as a doctrine which cannot be overemphasized. The Marxian Communist in proclaiming economic circumstance to be everything in forming a culture does not disguise his open and emphatic materialism.

This second postulate, that religion is the making of a culture, will upon a sufficient examination, I think, be granted; and if it is at first unfamiliar and therefore doubted, that is because we are accustomed to think of religion as a private matter, whereas, in social fact, it is a public one. Things really held to be sacred are held sacred throughout the society which is affected by them.

My third postulate is that the evidence on which we base our historical conclusion must include much more than documents; much more than recorded statements. We have also tradition. Memories passed on from one generation to another tend of course to be distorted, and if they are written down very late will often contain false elements of mere legend. But, on the other hand, tradition is sincere (which the written evidence of one witness very often is not) and it is broad-based. Over and over again a tradition which the learned, depending upon documents alone have ridiculed, turns out upon the discovery of further corroboration to be true.

Thus after all the guess-work and various readings of the Homeric poems, recenty discovered papyri in general confirm the traditional readings. Or again, there remained for centuries in the popular speech of Paris the term "araines" (variously and later spelled—"arenes"), attaching to a particular quarter of the town. Learned guess-work did its best with that term and could make little of it; what was at any rate generally agreed upon was that it could have nothing to do with the Roman word "arena," because there was no trace of a Roman amphitheatre in Paris. Well, in quite modern times during the construction of the Rue Monge, the foundations of the first tiers of such an amphitheatre were laid bare; and popular tradition thus confirmed.

These are only two instances where a hundred could be cited by any widely read man from memory alone; and a thousand or more could be established by research.

This postulate, warning us against the now happily decreasing tendency to base all history upon document alone, is especially confirmed by the growth in importance of archæology in recent years.

Then there is the evidence of common sense, that is, the nature of things. No matter how strong the tradition or how emphatic and well supported the documentary evidence, one must weigh against it the mere material possibility of this or that—for instance, the population which can possibly have inhabited a given area, the number of combatants that can possibly have occupied a particular line of battle, the time in which a sailing boat—however fiercely driven—can have covered a particular distance. History swarms with examples of particular statements, traditional and documentary, which are not indeed to be denied entirely, but to be modified by the use of mere reason and experience in this fashion.

Lastly there is a fourth postulate against which a modern audience must be warned more than an audience of earlier times would need to have been. This is that one must never regard an historical statement as being mere advocacy unless we have reasons in the statement for thinking so.

Today men always say, "So-and-so, *though* of such and such an opinion, admits . . . etc." Or again, "Even the historian So-and-so, *though* himself a Russian" (or an Italian, or what not), "considers . . . etc." These phrases and hundreds of others like them all imply that the historian in question is talking to a brief and presents a picture in order to make that brief good. But as a fact the recognition of reality, the discovery of what really happened and its quality is an occupation so fascinating and absorbing that one may properly allow it to outweigh affection in the mind of the narrator. The discovery of truth is in itself a delight, and to this may be added the most important fact that such and such an historical truth remains true whether the man appreciating it is in sympathy or not. The Pagan who describes the advance of the Church in the 4th century—the biographer of Julian the Apostate, for instance—and his contemporary who exults in the triumph of the Church and the defeat of Paganism are both stating a plain historical fact, that Paganism receded and the Catholic Church advanced between the years 300 and 400 A.D. An indifferent observer who cared for neither Paganism nor the Church would equally acknowledge that established truth.

The wise reader of history is he who can so detach himself as to say, "This happened, and it happened thus. I will describe it as though I cared nothing one way or the other." He may indeed care passionately; he may deplore as an awful tragedy or applaud as a glorious triumph the same event: history as such should care nothing for his applause or his grief, it is concerned only with the establishment of what *was*.

Armed with such principles let us begin our study of that great affair: "What we of Christendom are and how we came to be so."

We are studying an organism, to wit our civilization, Christendom. We are occupied in appreciating its nature, the spirit by which it lived and was maintained for so many centuries; we are doing this further to understand its breakdown today and the consequent mortal peril in which we lie.

Now in studying an organism it is essential to begin by appreciating its origins. It is both a truth and a commonplace that to understand a human character you must know the influences that came upon it in very early youth, during the "formative period." The same is true of a State, a polity, a nation; a general culture. And it is profoundly true of Christendom. Christendom arose upon a certain foundation which becoming alive, changed from a foundation to a root. Our origin appears in a certain arrangement of human Society whence we all descend; a great united State to which all that we do and think of any consequence refers as a beginning.

That vast State was called historically the Roman Empire; a more accurate term and one now increasingly used is the Græco-Roman Empire; for the language, local religion and literature of the educated classes and officials and even in actual numbers of the bulk of the people was the Roman speech (that is Latin), in the West, and the Greek speech in the East. The influences connected with those two idioms, Roman law, Greek philosophy and letters, were closely intermixed throughout the whole. Every Latin-speaking man of high social position was trained in the use of the Greek tongue, which for the more cultivated was as familiar as his own. It is not equally true that the Greek-speaking part of the Empire was intimately familiar with Latin, for Greek was regarded by both parties as the superior form of culture and every administrator within the Greek-speaking half of the Empire had come to take Roman law and the Roman discipline as a matter of course.

This great united State within which there were no customs, boundaries nor national frontiers, but which was all one political thing, covered the districts we now call Belgium and most of Holland, France, Italy, Spain and Portugal, all North Africa lying between the desert and the Mediterranean, what we now call Greece and the Balkan States, most of Austria, Turkey and Asia Minor, most of Syria. All these became in political life one nation, the area of which measured well over 2000 miles from east to west and at its broadest part between the mouths of the Rhine and the Sahara over a thousand. The thing had taken on this shape and unity in final form a lifetime before the Incarnation of Our Lord; but it had not settled down so early into an accepted general base. Rival claimants for power each using armed forces at their disposal and rival factions within the central power of Rome kept it fluctuating within and its fate uncertain until nineteen years before the beginning of our era.

The Eastern, which was also roughly the Greek half of this immense territory, was the more thickly populated;

and the wealthiest; the Western half had on the whole the greater dignity because it contained and was especially moulded by the City of Rome, whence the government of the whole from east to west and north to south had spread in the course of the preceding three or four centuries.

The dividing lines between the Western and Eastern halves was the Adriatic Sea and the tangle of mountains between the head of that sea and the Danube. The only land frontiers of the great thing were two rivers, the course of the Rhine on the east following the river up the first two-thirds of its length, then cutting across the upper third of the Danube, thence running down the Danube to the Black Sea. Beyond this line were tribes and clans who spoke Germanic and Slavonic dialects, but had no political cohesion; they fell naturally more and more under the influence of the civilized imperial society according as they lived nearer to the Rhine and the Danube, and had more intercourse with the soldiers and citizens and merchants of the Empire. There was no hostility or ill feeling between the organized and civilized society within the boundaries and the less and less organized, more and more barbaric outside. There was some pressure from outside which took the form of occasional raids, or even of large armed incursion. That was inevitable because the outer men naturally desired to enjoy the greater amenities of life within the frontiers of civilization. There was also equally inevitably a drift of outer men seeking better fortune through recruitment in the Imperial Army or private services, or through a sort of colonization of the imperial lands where they were permitted to settle and no small infiltration through commerce, including the trade in slaves; but it is important for us to see the Græco-Roman Empire of this period, just before our era, and on for generations, not as a sharply distinct civilized thing surrounded by mere barbarism, but as an influence which more and more affected the populations outside its political boundaries, and in its turn was affected by them through an admixture of external blood. From the beginning you find plenty of outer men as soldiers and slaves and even as settlers, let alone as visitors of consequence among the citizens of the Empire, whether in origin they were from Celtic or Slav or German clans outside the strictly defined frontier. Similarly you could find merchants travelling from within the frontier to places as far as the Baltic.

Although, as I have said, two main official languages dominated East and West of this single state, Greek and Latin, there were a considerable number of major language groups different from both, and innumerable lesser dialects spoken.

The State was not centralized in our modern sense; its social arrangements were freer than we know today. Localities were subject (save in major matters) to local administration alone; magistrates were often elected and always in tune with local feeling and usually native as well, though there were put over large districts as governors, officials appointed by the main council of the Roman State—the Senate—and the chief of the Roman executive, the Emperor.

In what we call today Tunis the language most spoken by the people was Semitic of a sort called "Punic," from its Phœnician origins. Further west along the southern coast of the Mediterranean, up to and including Morocco and the town of Tangier, the local dialects were probably Berber. Within what is now Spain and Portugal, Iberian idioms were spoken. In what is today France and most of Belgium, Celtic idioms survived, though these were to die out rapidly under the influence of Rome, a sort of popular Latin taking their place. All along the Rhine in a broad belt the citizens of the Empire spoke various Teutonic (that is Germanic) tongues, as they did presumably along the Danube, and certainly within the frontiers between the upper courses of those two rivers. In Asia Minor there were many idioms spoken, including a relic of Gaulish Celtic, remaining like a fossil from earlier Gallic invasions which had reached thus far eastward. The Delta and the Valley of the Nile were, as far as the population went, Coptic in speech, that is, using an idiom drawn from the ancient Egyptian tongue, though the ruling families spoke Greek. Similarly along the Syrian seacoast, including Palestine and all the belt between Syria and the Mediterranian, varieties of local languages (nearly all of them Semitic in character) were the habitual speech of the people. There is one particularly important to the story of our civilization—Hebrew—in its later form Aramaic, which was talked in Jerusalem, Galilee and all that we later came to call the Holy Land. It was probably the tongue in which Our Lord Himself and His Apostles spoke, though they must certainly have been acquainted with Greek also and have used it when a wide audience was being appealed to, for Greek was the cultivated and written language of Palestine.

It should be noted that though there was no political hostility, no conscious feeling of national or racial enmity along the enormously long frontiers of the Empire, there was one sector where such enmity and permanent political conflict could be found; that was the fluctuating frontier between the Roman Empire and the Asiatic and Persian power. Rome occasionally pushed as far as the Euphrates and even to the Tigris; the Persian power representing Asia and its hostility to the European would thrust back the Roman power at intervals to the Syrian desert and even later make incursions as far as the Mediterranean seaboard. It was upon this frontier alone that Rome feared invasion and influences destructive of all Greek and Latin culture. For the rest, there was either peace (and peace endured for long periods and was for generations the normal product of united government, which protected by its army all that lay within the frontiers), or where there were raids across the frontiers and the menace of raids, such fighting as took place was police work rather than war.

This enormous Græco-Roman State and culture had been built up by the coalescence of a number of diverse city-states and lesser kingdoms rather than by conquest. We must not imagine Roman armies proceeding from the City of Rome and gradually subduing all Western human-ity by force until all obeyed the master of those armies resident in the central town of Rome itself. That is a way in which the thing is so often regarded and it is thoroughly unhistorical. The Græco-Roman Empire had grown, it had not been artificially or mechanically *made,* although in step after step of this growth military action had come in to consolidate the results of such growth or secure it from disorder.

In Italy the thing had been begun by the town of Rome, a large central market fixed at an essential nodal point in the communications of the peninsula; the point where the first bridge crossed the main river of the eastern Italian seaboard. The inhabitants of that district had petty skir-mishes with their neighbors and also alliances with them; these feuds and treaties and commercial arrangements resulted in a sort of small central State occupying the fertile land between the Apennines and the sea. The prin-ciple of coalescence, including the further recruitment of the expanding citizenry into any army which had originally been but a militia of Romans, continued until all Italy south of the Po was directly or indirectly involved in it. Greek colonies to the south joined the union or fought against it and were subdued.

The irreducible foe of the whole movement was the very wealthy Semitic Society of Carthage, replaced today by the neighboring capital of Tunis in North Africa. Carthage depended upon sea power and upon its incalculable wealth, that of a mercantile aristocratic banking state. All its morals and ideas were in acute antagonism to those of our race: and Rome entered into a struggle with Carthage wherein the latter was destroyed. Meanwhile the Greek civilization had also coalesced, their unity springing from original efforts which had repelled the Orientals and their attempted invasion of the European mainland. The Greek culture was gathered under the rule of an outer province thereof, Macedonia, to the north: A young King of Macedonia with a small Greek expeditionary force had swept through the near East and suddenly planted the Greek language and influence and ideas upon all the eastern shores of the Mediterranean, and far inland as well. His armies even reached the river Indus, and when he died as quite a young man (little more than thirty), though his empire was divided among his generals, its spiritual unity as a Greek thing survived.

Rome in eliminating Carthage had come into possession of the islands of the western Mediterranean and ultimately most of what is today Spain and North Africa; her armies were superior to the Greek-speaking armies now orientalized and therefore recruited from inferior material; she entered into the inheritance of Alexander and his successors, but she entered into them not as an enemy, but respectfully, as a spiritual ally and even as a pupil—of such prestige was the philosophy and spiritual tradition of Hellas, as the Greek race called the Greek land, its original home.

Thus it was that the universal Mediterranean State, the Græco-Roman Empire, expanded, consolidated and was fixed, until, as I have said, half a lifetime before the birth of Our Lord, universal peace and a consolidated State lay over all the known Western World.

The framework of all that society was, from the nature of its expansion, the army. The idea of a State dependent on its army is unfamiliar to us today, but one that seemed to the men of the time the most natural in the world. The Roman army, which was of course, no longer composed of Romans or even of Italians for the most part, but recruited from the whole territory, was the cement of the whole structure. Its engineers planned the great roads which bound the Empire together; it was the principle of order and discipline which informed the whole. Its commander-in-chief was the head of the State. It is from that title, "Commander-in-Chief" that we get the word "Emperor," which is but our modern derivative of the Latin name for a commander-in-chief: "Imperator."

We have noted that this universal government of the West exerted but little or no pressure upon private life. There was none of that detailed interference with men which the modern State has so strictly developed. All that the State was concerned to do was to impose major rules for the guidance of the Courts of Law, especially in matters of property and contract; to prevent private war and brigandage. As for opinion, even in the form of intense religious feeling, that was free so long as it did not challenge the State. Only certain practices abhorrent to the conscience of our race and the high civilization of Greece and Rome—such as human sacrifice, the vilest product of the Carthaginian religion—were put down.

For the rest, the philosophy or general religion which ran through the whole political body was a complex of myths, varying liturgies and worships, societies professing to move spiritual aid by initiation, and therefore perform mysteries. Various powerful schools of thought upon the nature of the universe, most of them Greek in origin, formed cross sections in all this. There was the Epicurean school, very nearly what we call today Materialists; the Platonic, which was conscious of and relied upon spiritual reality; even the Cynics, who gave up any moral effort as hopeless of achievement. All these and any other opinions had free course; the worship of the local gods in each city-state was carried on under the protection of the local government; the strange rites of Egypt, the special ceremonies of the Syrian cities, and even the recalcitrant assertive special religious organization of the Jews, which last were at their most vital in their original homeland, the limestone hills of Judea with the national temple at Jerusalem, but also dispersed far and wide with the Jewish merchants and money-dealers all over the Empire, with their synagogues in most of the main cities, and very numerous in Rome, most numerous of all in the main Mediterranean port of Alexander—all were tolerated.

The influence both of Greek philosophy and Roman law made for the acceptation throughout this wide political body, the Empire, of what is called in our theology "natural religion"; the institution of the family with its loyalties and disciplines, therefore of marriage, of property whereby the freedom and secure existence of the family is maintained; the duty of maintaining social order —all that makes up, apart from revelation the duty of man, as the instincts of our race sees that duty, and indeed as we may fairly say humanity at large, save for a few exceptions sees it also. As for a common worship there was none, save a very vague and formal recognition of something divine about public authority as centered in the Emperor, and a kind of divine mission attached to the town of Rome itself: "The Goddess Rome," later on, "The Divine Emperor." Such phrases connoted some very shadowy concept of religious feeling common to the whole Empire; they did not intimately affect the lives of men, which in so far as they were touched by religion at all were touched only by decaying ancestral myths, more vigorous (because more modern) philosophies, and popular, domestic, local idolatries.

It is natural for us after generations and centuries of Christian formation to ask, "Had they no sense of immortality; did they not look to rewards and punishments in a future life to compensate for the inequalities and injustices of this world?" The answer to that question is that there was some such sentiment abroad, but nowhere very vital or active. The Egyptians seem to have had (for their wealthier classes at least and in the custody of their strict priesthood) an elaborate paraphernalia recognizing the survival of the soul. In Etruria the tombs —of the governing class at least—bear witness to the same. One section and one section only of Greek philosophy inclined to similar ideas; but nowhere was immortality, least of all in the form of vivid and certain expectation, a part of the popular mind. In so far as that mind contemplated the fate of the dead at all, it thought of their continuation as something tenuous, ex-sanguine, weak and most pitiable, presumably evanescent.

When we turn from the general philosophy (which is the determining element in every Society) to the social state accompanying it, we discover one most characteristic difference between that ancient world and our own; that difference is the universal presence of *slavery* as the economic basis of Society. Slavery was not peculiar to the Græco-Roman world. It was present among the less civilized clans and tribes outside as well, it was everywhere. At first, no doubt, as in the case of our own wage-system, it was mainly a domestic, familiar and tolerable thing; but it became, as Society grew, both more united and more complex; a mechanical and oppressive burden weighing upon the human spirit and giving a certain savor to those who were bondsmen, for all Society is affected by the spirit of any part thereof.

Politically the organization of all that world was a general monarchy, the rules of the civil service of which were upon a model mainly taken from the immensely older, highly organized, very wealthy state of Egypt. For all local affairs the spirit was rather that of oligarchy, administration in the hands of local magnates for lesser affairs, for the small communities a spirit almost what we should call today democratic. But the Structure, the stuff of Society, which, in importance, over-rides mere political arrangement, was based upon and rooted in slavery. The harder work of the world was done under compulsion; not under indirect compulsion—physical pain and death for the slave who did not accomplish his task, imposed upon him by the will of another man, his master.

What was the major spiritual result of all these things combined? Of a universal state through which great numbers moved without restriction, plying their commerce, ordering the army in its marches, travelling from curiosity or for betterment, but everywhere interchanging ideas and learning thereby to doubt ancestral habits and experience things foreign and therefore difficult of assimilation? What was the major note running through this high pagan world, with all its splendor and all its noble appreciation of beauty and order?

It was despair. The further that civilization proceeds in its development—a rapid development changing it and ageing it within three centuries—the more this mixture of despair penetrates it. You feel it in the growing lethargy of men's action; in the sterilization of their inventive power, and most of all in the continuous note of their highest letters. The greatest verse is filled with what a modern poet has excellently called in the English language "the doubtful doom of humankind," the irretrievable, and the certitude that none return from the dead.

Of a thousand superb lines which might be chosen to illustrate the profundity of this abandonment, remember these from the greatest of all the Latin poets:

"Soles redere et occidere possunt
Nobis cum semel occidit brevis lux
Nox est perpetua una dormiunda."*

It is the cry of Catullus. The Græco-Roman society was dying of old age, but to say that is only to say half and the less important half of the truth; the other half of the truth is that it was dying in despair, when there arrived slowly to permeate it a force whereby it was transformed.

As we approach the conversion of the Roman Empire (A.D. 29-33 to A.D. 500), we come upon a moment of history so surpassing, in its value and effects, all others known to us that we must begin by standing apart and contemplating its magnitude. That is the essential in the attitude to be taken by anyone who cares for reality in history. It was not an episode among the great episodes of our race; it was not a chapter, the greatest chapter of many, it was the Determining Thing. It was not only in scale but in quality Creation.

This is true quite apart from the standing question, whether that revolution in the human mind were an illusion or a revelation of reality. A man concerned with the story of his ancestry on this earth may condemn the great change as a false turning, a warping of values, a lamentable lessening of intelligence, or he may acclaim it as a

---

* This has been translated:
"Suns may set and suns may rise,
Our poor eyes,
When their little light is past,
Droop and go to sleep at last."

vision of reality whereby the world was and can be saved. Whether he passionately approve or hate the event (as most men will who do not approve it), it remains an historical fact that no such construction has to our knowledge appeared before or since. Certainly unique in character, it is also unique in scale or rather is of another kind from any other production or formation of the human spirit. For whether the momentous change of our Fathers from pagan to Christian were man-made, or given to man by Divine influence from above, it remains in either case unique: something quite by itself and producing effects not comparable to those of any other cause.

We must begin by laying it down, again as an historical fact, not to be removed by affection one way or the other, that the conversion of the Roman Empire was a conversion to what was called by all our ancestry and what is still called by those with any just historical sense, the Catholic Church.

The Empire was *not* converted to what modern men mean when they used the word "Christianity." The phrase is continually used and as continually corrupts the historical judgment of those who use it and those who hear it. In the ears of modern youth, especially in societies which have lost the Catholic culture, the word "Christianity" means vaguely, "That which is common to the various sects, opinions and moods inherited in diluted form from the Reformation." In England today for instance, "Christianity" means a general feeling of kindliness—particularly to animals. To some more precise in mind it may mean an appreciation of, and even an attempt at copying, a Character which seems to them portrayed in the four Gospels (four out of certainly more than fifty, which four they happen to have inherited from the Catholic Church—although they do not know it). To a much smaller number, with greater powers of definition and better historical

instruction, the word "Christianity" may have even so
precise a meaning as "the acceptation of the doctrine that
an historical Figure appeared in Palestine not quite two
thousand years ago, and was in some way the Incarnation
of God, and that the main precepts, at least, of an original
society calling itself after His name should be our guide
for moral conduct."

But all these uses of the word "Christianity" from the
vaguest to the most precise, do not apply to the tremendous
business with which we are here concerned. The society of
the ancient world was not changed from its antique attitude to that which it finally adopted in the 4th century (and
continued thenceforward to spread throughout Europe)
by any mood or opinion; it was transformed by adherence
to the doctrine and discipline as well as the spirit and
character of a certain *institution;* and that *institution* is
historically known; it is a Personality which can be tested
by certain indisputable attributes, practices and definitions.
It claimed and claims Divine authority to teach, to include
in its membership by a specific form of initiation those
who approached it and were found worthy; to exclude
those who would not accept that unity and supremacy.
It performed throughout the society of the Empire and
even beyond its boundaries a certain liturgical act of sacrifice, the Eucharist, it affirmed its foundation by a Divine
figure who was also a man, and a manifestation of God.
It further affirmed that its officers held their authority
through appointment originally by this Founder, who
gathered a small group for that purpose; it affirmed that
from the members of this small original group, in unbroken
succession, descended the spiritual powers which could be
claimed by officers and by them alone, in a particular manner, over the whole body of Christians, and, in general
fashion, over the world at large.

In order to understand this very great thing which captured and transformed the old pagan world we must grasp its nature. We must be able to answer the question, *"What was it that spread thus so rapidly and so triumphantly throughout the Græco-Roman world?"* Secondly, we must appreciate the *method* by which this revolution was accomplished; lastly, in order to understand both the nature and the method of the thing we must discover why it met with so intense a *resistance,* for that resistance explains both its character and its ways of propagation—and it was victory over that resistance which established the Catholic Faith and practice so firmly over our race for so many centuries and generations.

First then, as to the nature of the conquest. The great change did not come because "it met a need"; it did indeed meet needs that were universal. It filled up that aching void in the soul which was the prime malady of the dying ancient society, also it relieved and dissipated despair, the capital burden imposed by that void.

Yet the meeting of the need was not the essential character of the new thing; it was not the driving power behind the great change; it was only a result incidental thereto.

It was not merely in order to assuage such needs of the spirit that men turned towards the Catholic Church: had that been so we should have been able to trace the steps whereby from vague gropings and half-satisfied longings there should have crystalized this and that myth, this and that fulfilment of desire by imagination, until the system should have come into being long after the inception of the first influences.

That such a gradual process did take place is commonly affirmed by those who have not a sufficient acquaintance, even on the largest lines, with the thing historically—but in fact nothing of the kind took place. You discover not a vague frame of mind, but a definite society from the first; no criticism of documents or of tradition can present any

other conclusion. A man appeared, gathered together a
certain company and taught. And not only so soon as that
company begins to act, but at the root of all memory with
regard to its action, you have the specific claim of Divine
revelation in the Teacher, of His Human and Divine
nature; of His resurrection from the dead; of His estab-
lishing a central rite of Sacrifice, which was called the
Eucharist (the Act of Gratitude); the claim to authority;
the Apostolic organization of the tradition; the presence
of a hierarchy—and all the rest.

The Catholic Church visible was not an influence that
spread; it was a Thing. It was fixed Corporation, a Club,
if you will; it was an organization with a form and members, a defined outline, and a discipline. Disputes arose
within it, certain of its members would overemphasize this
or that among the doctrines for which it stood, and so
warp the proportion of the whole.

But no innovator, even during the first enthusiasm when
so many debates surrounded so intellectually vigorous a
thing, would ever pretend that there was not one body
to be preserved. He might claim to be the true continuator
of that body, and protest (when he was excluded from it
for dissent); but never did any one of those at the origin
propose that discord upon essentials could be permanent.

This new and strict corporation had a name, a name
associated in the minds of its contemporaries with the idea
of a secret society possessed of mysteries; it called itself
the EKKLESIA.* Now it is all-important to grasp this

---

* This Greek word means literally "an assembly." But there were many
Greek terms for an assembly; and *this* term EKKLESIA had long been
used for an assembly closed and compact; especially a secret one for the
celebration of mysteries. And it is from this word that we get the French
"eglise," the Welsh "eglwys," the Italian "chiesa," etc. The word
"church" came round through the missionaries who spread the Faith in
the north; the other form, "kirk," is thought to be derived from
"kyriakon," "the Lord's house," but more probably from "kirkle," "a
circle," or, "a group."

further fact, that the new Ekklesia with its mysteries, its initiation ceremonies (instruction in doctrine, solemn affirmation thereof, called a "confession"—what today we call a creed—and Baptism) was not one of many religions which happened to prove the winner in a sort of race. That is an error which one finds in many of the textbooks and which has almost passed into popular acceptance. Any number of our general outlines of history and the rest talk of the Early Church in this fashion.

They say, for instance, that the earlier mysteries such as the mysteries of Eleusis, the later mysteries of Mithras, and the Egyptian mysteries of Isis, etc., were of this sort and what they call "Christianity" (for they usually avoid the word "Catholic Church") was but one of many.

This is not true, and the test that it is not true is simple and should be conclusive. The Catholic Church alone and from its origins proclaimed the Divinity of a real historical man and the objective truth of the doctrines which it affirmed. It proclaimed from the beginning the Resurrection of that real historical man from the dead; and the popular nickname, "Christian" (which became like so many nicknames the general term) arose from that fact.

All the other popular worships with their mysteries and initiations and the rest of it were admittedly *myths*. They did not say, "This happened"; what they said was, "This is a parable, a symbol to explain to you the nature and possible fate of the human soul and its relation to the Divine." Not one of them said, "I was founded by a real man whom other men met and knew, who lived in a particular place and time, one to whom there are 'a cloud of witnesses'"; not one of them said that they held revealed truth and that their officials held a Divine communion to explain that truth throughout the world.

In all this there was a violent contrast between the Catholic Church and the whole of the pagan world around;

neither the intellectuals following Greek traditions nor the Roman Empire with its administrative sense of unity persecuted the other associations. It was not the doctrine of the Resurrection, still less the doctrine of Immortality which was found repulsive; it was the affirmation that the criminal who had been put to death in a known place and time at Jerusalem, under the Emperor Tiberius, condemned to scourging and the ignominious capital punishment of Crucifixion, whereto no Roman citizen was liable, was Divine, spoke with Divine authority, founded a Divine Society, rose from the dead, and could promise to his faithful followers eternal beatitude. This was what shocked the intellectuals, but this also was what gave stuff and substance to that new society and so led as we shall see in a moment to persecution.

Now, as to its method of expansion, how did it propagate itself? What was the machinery which proved so successful that in less than four long lifetimes the whole of that hostile society was officially Catholic, and that within another two long lifetimes the whole of the population, West and East, of the known world between the Channel, the Rhine, the Danube and the desert followed its creed and accepted its doctrines?

It worked by the method which we have come to call "Cells," a word rendered familiar today through the universal Communist agitation. If, as some think, that Communist movement is the final assault upon Catholic tradition and the Faith, if it be, as many think, the modern anti-Christ, the parallel is indeed striking. All over the Græco-Roman Empire there were founded rapidly a number of these small organizations, first connected with and later separated from local Jewish synagogues; fixed first in the greater towns, but later scattered like seed also in the provincial centers, and then by missionary effort throughout the countrysides.

We know that this was the method through ample documentary evidence; we have also a vast mass of tradition, largely legendary, of course, after such length of time, but containing its nucleus of truth, which tells us how in this place and in that these "Cells" were founded and established. Each was called individually a Church, just as the general organization was known as the Church as a whole. They were governed by a Hierarchy. At the head of one church would be one presiding officer, the Episkopos, a word of which we have made the English word "Bishop."

He was nominated sometimes, apparently by the local clergy, sometimes by the acclamation of the community; but he held his title not from these but from the Apostolical succession. This and that ancient local Church boasted that it had been founded by an Apostle, and soon in drawing up lists of Bishops the chain was traced to that Apostle who had first begun it by the laying on of hands. Those thus ordained would lay on hands in their turn, and so the hierarchy or body of the clergy was formed. After some indeterminate time not the Bishop alone (who was the full priest) but subordinates bearing the titles of "elders," in the Greek "presbuteros," could function at the Holy Mysteries, having been ordained in their turn by the Bishops. These consecrated the elements of the Eucharist, and from them would commonly be drawn the Episcopate. Such was the original form of the Church. The Ekklesia.

The Ekklesia had a body of writing which it preserved for the instruction of its members and the continuity of its doctrine; but it took a long time before these documents were sifted and before a certain proportion of them, a small portion of the whole, were affirmed to have special value as Scripture, that is, inspired and therefore authoritative. There were for instance in the way of records or pretended records of Our Lord's life and teaching certainly more than fifty such documents, for we have fragments of at least that number.

Only four were admitted to the Canon, that is, the "regular" or "official" collection. In the same way letters were written by the missionaries of the Early Church, but in the same way only a certain number, under the name of "Epistles," were admitted to the Canon, and one record of early Apostolic action, the Acts of the Apostles; one apocalyptical work, which we know as the Apocalypse.

This being the sequence whereby the Canon of what we call today the New Testament was gradually formed, (by selection over a long space of time) it is exceedingly bad history to pretend that this collection of documents was the authority for the Faith. The authority for the Faith was the tradition of the Apostles; the living agreement of the faithful, especially as represented by their heads in the Apostolic succession, the Bishops.*

Apart from this fundamental institution of the hierarchy, the sacred caste which alone had spiritual authority over the Church, there were four other elements which strengthened the new society and helped it to grow. There

---

* Although the word *Episkopos* means literally an overseer, and *presbuteros* means literally a senior, it is an ignorant error to think that this literal meaning was the original one. Episkopos was a word used with hieratic meaning in the mystery, presbuteros the same. The function of the Episkopos from the beginning, as we first find the word used by those who could remember the Apostles, was always that of a sacred ordained official in the Apostolic succession. And the other word no more meant *old in years* than the French word "seigneur," the Spanish "Señor," the Italian "Signore" mean *an old man*. These also all derive from the respectful term "senior." It is thought by some scholars that in some early cases a college or group of ordained men governed a particular church rather than an individual. The thing is obscure and doubtful, but, in any case, clearly exceptional; perhaps an interim arrangement pending an individual election. St. Ignatius of Antioch writes no further from Pentecost than we are from the Civil War in the United States. He writes in old age and his memory covered all the lifetime since the Crucifixion; and he takes personal monarchial episcopacy for granted, as does the tradition of every recorded City list.

was the function of intercommunication by travel and by correspondence, along the Imperial roads. All these Churches kept in touch and maintained a common doctrine alive. Councils of Bishops were held, (at least, after the Emperors had accepted the Catholic Church, and it had become the official religion). They would be summoned to represent the Church throughout the whole world, whence they derived their title "œcumenical."

The first of these, under the first Christian Emperor, Constantine, was summoned at Nicea near Constantinople because Constantinople had become the capital of the Empire. It met to discuss and define the full doctrine of Our Lord's Divinity, and to reject the heretical theses connected with it.

The function of getting into communication by travel and by letter supported and was called into being by the supreme principle of *Unity:* The idea that the Church was *one,* its doctrine one, its authority one, stood out vividly in the minds of all its members. From the beginning dissent was not tolerated; unity was of the essence of the thing, and in connection with this there was present at first more vaguely, later with greater definition, the conception of primacy. One of Our Lord's Apostles, Peter, was head of the Apostolic College; his See had a special, if at first less defined, position in Christendom; and Rome, where Peter was last settled, where he and Paul were martyred, became the permanent seat of this Primacy as it developed.

The third activity which made for the growing strength of the Church was the use of what we now call Creeds (from the Latin word, *"Credo,"* "I believe"). They were called in the East where Greek was spoken "symbols," from the Greek "symbolæ," which means things put together. They were originally called in the Latin-speaking West, "Confessiones." They arose in order to make sure that a new candidate for admission to the Ekklesia was not tainted with heresy. He or she was required before admission to recite truths which had been defined in order that such definition might combat false ideas. These brief recitals did not pretend to cover the Faith; they were not a summary of all, nor even of the principal, beliefs; for instance, the great creed of the 4th century made no mention of the most important and fundamental mystery of the new society, the Eucharist and the Real Presence of Christ therein. Of that doctrine there was ample evidence, going back to the beginning, but as it was not questioned its definition had never entered into these rebutting affirmations which the candidate was required to make.

The fourth function making for unity and strength and permanence and growth was, of course, that very Eucharist just mentioned. Bread and wine were consecrated after a method, and with words, handed down traditionally as those of Our Lord himself at the Last Supper. The mystic ceremony was performed by the celebrant hierarch, or hierarchs; on its performance the bread and wine over which the mystical formulæ had been uttered were believed to be no longer bread and wine but the Body and Blood of Christ Himself.

As St. Justin himself wrote, at a time which was to the Crucifixion as our time is to the Declaration of Independence, and writing as on a matter accepted and long established, writing moreover for the instruction of readers who were not Christian, the bread was no longer "common bread" but "the flesh of Christ."

All this gives us the external method and machinery whereby the Faith was established and spread with such astonishing success throughout a vast society which had begun by knowing it ill, had proceeded to hate it, and had at last accepted it for a universal religion.

But what was the internal force? How were men convinced? Why did they join this society in spite of the terrible risks communion with it involved? Often it meant ruin of fortune and thrusting out from the society of one's fellows and sometimes torture and death. What drove men to it? The answer is that the Church was a Person which men came to trust as they come to trust it today by experience: and having trusted, to love, as they love it today. A man became a Christian because he found that the Church affirmed things which he recognized to be true in experience and holy in character. It was loved, witnessed to and defended to the death by those who thus felt it to be, when in contact with it, divine, and the only fixed and certain divine authority of their experience. As for doctrine, they took it from this society of which they had thus become enamored upon such firm grounds. It was not the society which proceeded from the doctrine, but the doctrine that came from the society.

To understand this last point, which is fundamental to all comprehension of the Church's triumph over and penetration throughout the old Roman world, we must also understand the character of the violent resistance which it excited.

As that resistance is too often presented, it seems incomprehensible, because it is represented wrongly. People would not have been thrown to wild beasts, tortured to death, condemned to imprisonment with hard labor in the mines, simply because they preached a general spirit of kindliness, or worshipped a particular ideal Character. Nothing could have been more tolerant to opinion than the old Græco-Roman Empire. It is not true that the Empire persecuted the Church because it was a secret society. Mystery societies of various sorts flourished among the citizens; why then did an angry instinct for killing this particular one arise?

In some degree, no doubt, for that reason which we find hundreds of years before suggested by a Greek philosopher filled with vision. He wrote, that if humanity should come across a perfectly good man, his fellowmen would tear him to pieces. Holiness is a reproach. It was also persecuted perhaps because its claims and affirmations upon itself were novel. It said, as nothing else had yet said, "I am the voice of God. You must accept what I say as truth. My code of morals is the path to eternal beatitude and neglect or denial of them is the path to eternal despair." That was a challenge to all human custom; a sort of challenge not easily to be borne.

Allied to this was the hard, the angular quality of the new thing, with its strict definitions, its Hierarchy, its highly disciplined organization, standing thus as an alien body in the midst of a soft diliquescence: solid and with edges, in the midst of a society that was dissolving. It was an alien thing, and, as it were, indigestible; or rather it was something which had to be accepted altogether or crushed altogether, if there were to be any peace.

But there was a last political reason and a strong one for the resistance. As this highly organized definite, enthusiastic body spread, it became more and more a state within the State; it was a society with its own authorities, its own discipline and spirit in the midst of that Imperial World which was inspired by a political desire for general peace and unity. The Government of the Empire reacted inevitably and violently against the presence of such an opponent and challenger. It has been noted by many that the Emperors best at government were often the worst persecutors.

This resistance to the spread of the Faith, this compulsion laid upon the Catholic body to fight for its life, was a chief element in its final triumph. Permanent work is done in hard material. "Great sculpture is not fashioned in butter," as a just critic said of a minor poet's verses. The best carving is done in the closest-grained wood, and against the grain.

This great united state which included the whole of the known civilized world, the Græco-Roman Empire, fell at first gradually then more rapidly into a material decline.

All the first century and a half of our era, that is, more than a century and a half after the pacification and consolidation of the whole Empire under Augustus, its first monarch, the material decline was not apparent. In the earlier part of that period all civilization was at its height. The influence of Greek art perfected all that met the outward eye and literature still inherited the very high tradition of the Augustine period. The greatest names are found before or during the earlier part of those hundred and odd years.

But the outward character of civilization in letters as in everything else, in order, policing, law, road-making and building, remained at a summit. In general peace reigned, although there was occasional fighting between sections of the regular troops to decide who should be Commander-in-Chief, and therefore master of the State. Even on through the second century this order and peace continued, with its excellence in material civilization; though in some departments, for instance in sculpture and decoration there were signs of a baser and more mechanical spirit appearing. But after about three generations an appreciable decline appeared. It was no longer a threat or a beginning of decline but a manifest worsening of those things which mark a high civilization. Literary styles fell to a much lower level and continued to fall; architecture coarsened, advance in physical knowledge halted or went backward.

So long as what are known as the "Antonine Emperors"

held power things were well administered and though civilization was clearly on the downward grade no one felt the peril and it was not apparent. Many have said that this "Antonine Period" (from A.D. 98 to A.D. 180) was the most secure and prosperous Europe had hitherto known, although the arts were certainly already failing.

But after the Antonines things began to break down. The last but one of those Emperors, the scholarly but weak Emperor-philosopher, Marcus Aurelius, the dupe of his wife, nominated his own son to succeed him. Hitherto it had been the rule of the Antonine period for each Emperor to nominate his successor, chosen for his ability to command soldiers and to govern the State on its civil side as well. That rule was now broken, Marcus Aurelius' son was quite unworthy of his position and his reign was the approach of a welter in which authority was weakened. The middle of the third century was a time in which all manner of upstart soldiers took over government, each in his own region and over his own troops; there was a sort of moral anarchy in which the prestige of the Imperial Roman Government sank low.

Meanwhile there were recurrent and increasing economic crises; money was debased, all the machinery for trade and production got out of gear. It was clear to every observer that our civilization had gone down a great step to a lower level and threatened to sink further still. The main function of the Army, the saving of the civilized and wealthy part of Europe from raids by the half-civilized people beyond the frontiers, was ill conducted; the security of the frontier regions grew less, the anxiety for their future grew greater.

Order was restored by a Commander-in-Chief called Aurelian, who might be named the second founder of the Imperial scheme. But it was most noticeable that even as he and his immediate successors pursued their task of setting things to rights again the whole of Society appeared transformed and transformed for the worse. Art had quite palpably declined, and literature with it. The Empire during the worst of its troubles had shown great powers of survival; Europe remained coherent, the Græco-Roman culture though it had been degraded did not perish. The raids of pirates upon the coast and of marauding bands over the frontiers were not allowed to inflict damage beyond a certain measure; our civilization lowered though it was in intellectual and esthetic tone still seemed secure and immutable.

None the less decline continued. At the end of the third century a very remarkable soldier and administrator, the Emperor Diocletian, attempted a reorganization of the whole State and many of the divisions he laid down lasted for centuries. The provinces which he defined remained marked by the same limits right on until the Middle Ages and many of them much later still. In a number of cases our ecclesiastical dioceses coresponded for centuries to these divisions.

The framework of the Empire stood; its coinage, its laws, all its life moved on without a break. There was no "Fall of the Roman Empire"—the phrase is rhetorical and false; but there *was* a profound change proceeding in the texture of Society. The half-civilized tribes on the fringes of the Empire filtered in more and more into Græco-Roman society, acquired more power and introduced elements of disorder; the ruling class changed and largely lost its culture.

On the material side of life all seemed to be sinking slowly, even while on the spiritual side there was rising to triumph the mighty force of the Catholic Church.

Now since the rise of the one spiritual thing and the fall of the other material thing were coincident, may not they be related as cause and effect?

This is the capital question which we have to deal with on approaching the decline of the Roman Empire in material things.

The answer was given without hesitation by the scholars of the Renaissance who rediscovered the glories of pagan antiquity and themselves became half pagan in spirit. They often said, they always implied, that what ruined the material civilization of the old Græco-Roman Empire, that glorious pagan civilization of the statues and the colonnades, the high verse and the high philosophy, was the spread of a superstition, of something degrading: The spread of that which those who do not know the Faith call "Christianity," but which those who know the Faith call by its right name, the Catholic Church.

While the Empire was changing under the growing influence of the Church, contemporary witnesses said exactly the same thing. The chronicler of the pagan re-action under Julian the Apostate half a lifetime after the victory of Constantine, wrote, "The Christians, to whom we owe all our misfortunes. . . ."

That the enemies of the Church or those who know the Church imperfectly or those who, like the scholars of the Renaissance, were in reaction against the Church should have spoken thus, is comprehensible. Much more remarkable is the fact that the defenders of the Church, in the last four hundred years have reëchoed that same complaint though in a different form.

"Yes," they say, "material civilization did decline as the Empire turned Christian; the Dark Ages did coincide with the triumph of the Faith. But why? Because men's minds were naturally turned, during the disasters of human society, to the consolation of Divine things. What matter if somewhat less attention were paid to art and letters and if the stuff of Society coarsened, so long as a spiritual advantage of supreme value was gaining ground all the time?"

That sort of attitude went on until past the middle of the 19th century, the enemies of the Faith making certain that history proved this breakdown of civilization to be due to the spread of Oriental superstitions, especially the superstition of the "Ekklesia." The Catholics often reluctantly admitted the same thesis—they who should have known better. They excused the coincidence between Catholic victory and decay in architecture, sculpture, history, verse and the rest, by saying that it did not matter since at last Divine things had come down to men. The price, they said, was worth the paying.

But the truth of the business, which people only began to recover within living memory (because only within living memory has history been fully examined and scientifically treated) is almost the opposite of what had been said so long. It was not the spread of the Faith which undermined the high civilization of pagan antiquity; on the contrary, the Faith saved all that could be saved; and, but for the conversion of the Roman Empire, nothing of our culture would have remained.

That truth had already been put in one sentence by St. Jerome when he said, that if the Græco-Roman world had accepted the Catholic Church in time the decay of civilization would never have taken place.

The dates are sufficient proof in this matter. The old pagan civilization was in active decay long before the new small and struggling obscure group of Catholic congregations began to have any appreciable effect. The golden age of literature was passed, letters had become sterile, architecture coarsened, long before the Ekklesia was felt to be a menacing force to the natural Paganism of the Old World. Already old age, corruption, greed, the preponderance of slaves and "Freed-men"* side by side with the growth of vast fortunes overshadowing Society and throwing it out of balance, had already been at work when the Catholic Church was still so insignificant that it is hardly mentioned by the mass of contemporary writers. There are one or two allusions here and there which have reference to this body, but no more. Only when the Empire was *already* almost broken down, in the 3rd century, does the Church begin to make a strong appeal; and even then its members were as yet but a small minority even in the East. They were a still smaller minority in the West.

Nor were Christians found in any of the principal places of authority; nor possessing power through wealth, still less through office. Tertullian had said at the beginning of the grave social crisis that all might be well if the Cæsars could be Christian—but took it for granted that the Cæsars could not be Christian.

It is more than a coincidence that the triumph of the Catholic Church came at last coincidently with the restoration of order.

The reëstablishment of Imperial administration, arms and general obedience in the later part of the 3rd century, with the growing appeal of the Catholic lucidity and discipline is not fortuitous. The fact that when one man at last became the monarch of the world, Constantine, he also recognized and promoted what was to be the world-religion is not an accident; the two things were the fruit of one spirit running through Society. The Græco-Roman world not only needed inspiration and vision which had died within it but needed also unity, and the principle of certitude without which unity cannot be.

I repeat that central phrase, for it is fundamental to

---

* A "Freed-man" was a slave whom his master had emancipated but who still owed devotion and service.

the whole story; so far from the Church causing the decline of Society under which the old Empire slipped into the Dark Ages, the Church saved all that could be saved.

Amid the decline there had come as a contributory cause a sort of social revolution due to the change in the character of the Army.

The old Roman State, be it remembered, was based on the Army; the Army was its cement, and, one might almost say, its principle of being. That is why, as we have seen, the head of the State was Head of the State, because he was Head of the Army: that is why we talk of an "Emperor" instead of a King since the word "Emperor" (Imperator) means, as we have also seen, nothing more than head of the Army: "Commander-in-Chief."

Now the Roman Army which had begun by being a local Italian force and had later been recruited only from the people native to the Græco-Roman civilization (not only Gauls and Spaniards but also any material to be found among free men) gradually became formed of new material. The Roman citizens in the old sense of that term ceased to enlist in great numbers. With the world turned into one great state wherein local patriotism had disappeared, this mercenary professional army engaged mainly in police work, watching of the frontiers, did not appeal to the more fully civilized men. The armed strength of the Roman State came to depend more and more upon "Federate Troops," that is armed bodies of half-civilized men, who attracted by the luxury and amenities of the Roman towns would accept service under their own chiefs from the outer regions or were settled as defense-corps on the frontier lands.

These became more and more the stuff, the material of the Roman armies. They were in no way hostile to the civilization on the fringes on which they had always lived and within the frontiers of which many of them had been born. It was a civilization into which, as has been said in an earlier page, they had filtered continually, coming in not only as hired soldiers but as slaves or mere adventurers and settlers, or also as raiders.

With this changing of the stuff whereof the Roman Army was composed the whole of Roman society also changed; there was no conquest of the Empire by barbarians, there was an intermixture of soldiers from the half barbaric borders beyond the Roman line, an incorporation of an increasing number of half-civilized, but in the main Christian, men with the bulk of the citizens.

Under this change in the Army and in all Society the texture of the Græco-Roman world grew loose. It became more difficult than ever to maintain the traditions of a disciplined civil service; the Emperors had withdrawn to the East; the direct administration in Rome, in the West, became more difficult and at last it broke down altogether (though central power in Constantinople and the East still stood) where districts came to be governed by local Generals, who commanded soldiers recruited from the less civilized border clans. The authority of the Emperor was still recognized, though actual administrative power in Gaul and Italy and Spain and North Africa passed into the hands of the local troops and their chieftains, few in number, and for the most part Slav and Germanic. But be it remembered that these also were Christians and that for all of them the Empire represented the only civilization they knew, the only possible civilization, though they had unwittingly degraded it.

This change in the Army, this breakdown of Imperial local government in the West and the taking of it over by the commanders of garrisons often half-barbaric was a contributory cause to the sliding down of our civilization into the Dark Ages; but it was not the main cause. The main cause was that despair and senility into which the old pagan civilization had fallen long before and which the Church alone had power to revivify and in part to preserve.

Lastly, let it be remembered that though we must for the purposes of right history admit the continual material decline going on through those first five centuries during which the Empire turned from Pagan to Christian, the new religion brought with it invaluable compensations for evils which it had not caused but at the advance of which it had been present.

The Catholic Church brought to the old ruined, dying, despairing Græco-Roman world the quality of *vision*. It brought a motive for living and thence there came to it, sustaining all that could be sustained of that grievously weakened world, saner and more stable social arrangements.

The Catholic Church having become the religion of Græco-Roman society did among other things two capital things for the settlement of Europe on its political side, and for arresting the descent into chaos. It humanized slavery and it strengthened permanent marriage. Very slowly through the centuries those two influences were to produce the stable civilization of the Middle Ages, wherein the slave was no longer a slave but a peasant; and everywhere the family was the well-rooted and established unit of Society.

The old pagan world had reposed upon slavery, the great bulk of its human material was made up of slaves—perhaps two-thirds, perhaps more. The Catholic Church had grown up in that state of affairs; its members in the early centuries could conceive no other.

The Church never denied the right to own slaves, but it was the spirit of the Church which gradually transformed their condition. It became difficult, often impossible to deal with a baptized Christian man as a chattel; emancipation was fostered as a high act of charity. Under the first Christian Emperors the laws regulating the relations between slave and master grow continually more human.

Nor is it true that intellectual activity failed in the Dark Ages. What happened was that it changed its interests. There was a vast mass of writing, of eager disputation, but the matter of it was no longer doubtful, insoluble problems, disputations, an end to which was not expected or desired,—it dealt with certitude, with an ardent establishment of what it held to be an all-satisfying truth, the salvation of mankind and the defense of that truth against attack from without and from within.

It was long the fashion to deride the writings of the Fathers and all theological interest as foolish. In the English language that fashion is identified with the name of Gibbon, who drew all his inspiration and copied all his data from the anti-Catholic French writers of his day. But the Fathers, and indeed all those who took part in the vivid theological discussion which runs for generations and centuries through Europe, were at once conservative and creative; their intellectual energy saved us; their powers of definition and of appreciation are at the root of the culture which nourished Europe through the difficulties of the coming time—those centuries to which we shall next turn under the title of the "Siege of Christendom."

To sum up then, by the end of that great period, the first five centuries, extending from the Incarnation to the conversion of Clovis and the establishment of Catholic Gaul, the end of the five centuries during which all our ancestry turned from Paganism to Catholicism and during which the Empire was baptized, were centuries in which we suffered grave damage: disorder, barbarism threatening our race, the fall of the arts of great verse and of high unified administration, the worsening of roads, much loss of the knowledge inherited from the past (Greek for instance was dying out in the West and legend was more and more intermixed with real history). But Europe at that time was spiritually consolidated so that it proved able to meet and overcome the strain to which it was about to be subjected.

That strain would have come anyhow, the violent attack under which Europe nearly broke down, "The Siege of Christendom," was inevitable. But we survived it. Had it not been for the conversion of the world we should have gone under.

II

CHRISTENDOM ESTABLISHED

(a) THE SIEGE OF CHRISTENDOM

IN THE FORMATION of Christendom, its economic and social structure, under the influence of the Catholic Church, the next period after the first foundational one (of five hundred years) is another, also roughly of five hundred years: from approximately the year 500 to about the year 1000.

It is a period of five centuries—the 6th, 7th, 8th, 9th and 10th—which have commonly been called the "Dark Ages," but which may more properly be called "The Siege of Christendom." It was the period during which the Græco-Roman Empire, already transformed by Catholicism, fell into peril of destruction at the hands of exterior enemies. It was assaulted from the north, from the east, and from the southeast in two separate fashions. Hordes of wholly pagan barbarians, some issuing from Scandinavia, many Mongols, many Slavs, fiercely thrust at the boundaries of Christendom with the hope of looting it as their prey and therefore ruining it. These between them formed the eastern attack, coming from the districts we call today Sweeden and Norway and Denmark, Poland

and the Russian plains, Hungary and the Danube valley.

The struggle against these enemies of the Christian name and culture, who so nearly overwhelmed us, was at last successful. The siege was raised, we carried the influence of civilization outward among those who had been our savage opponents, and we ended by taming them all until they were incorporated into a new and expanded Christian civilization. That was the work of the Christian Church in the West, the Church under the direct authority of the Western Patriarch at Rome (who is also universal primate) and of the Latin liturgy.

What happened on the southeast was quite different. *There,* that is, against the Greek-speaking part of the Empire, directly ruled from Constantinople, the attack took the strange form of a sudden enthusiastic movement, which was both religious and military. It took the form of a swarm of light desert cavalry riding out from the sands of Arabia and swooping down on Greek-speaking and Greek-administered civilizations, Syria (including Palestine) and Mesopotamia, Egypt, and then from Egypt, following up all along the southern shores of the Mediterranean between the sea and the Sahara. It reached the Atlantic itself in Morocco, crossed the Straits of Gibraltar, and passed northward, overran Spain and even crossed the Pyrenees. To these mountains it was beaten back after its first northern extreme had been reached in the middle of France. This attack from the southeast was the Mahommedan attack, not pagan as was the other to the north, not savage, but, from the beginning, incorporating in its conquest all the elements of civilization, developing a high literature of its own, and turning at last from a heresy, which it was in its beginnings, to what was virtually a new religion and a new type of society —Islam.

The southeastern attack upon Christendom not only held its own but progressed with the centuries. It was indeed somewhat thrust back in Spain after many generations had passed, but it continued very strong all over North Africa and Syria; it ultimately swamped Constantinople itself, and, in quite modern times, less than a century before the Declaration of Independence, it threatened the capture of Vienna and the overwhelming of western Germany as well.

Let us look at this "Siege of Christendom" in somewhat more detail.

First, as to the northern and eastern attack, it was an attack by Scandinavia and the Baltic. It was essentially an attack by pirates few in number but very dangerous on account of their mobility and their fierce onslaught upon a decaying society; a society moreover, wherein the most of men were in servitude and could not be mobilized to defend the State, and where local governments were ill able to support each other on account of decay in the general organization, and central forces, of society. These pirate attacks had had a preliminary sort of rehearsal in the shape of what are loosely called the Saxon invasions of Britain, but what are really mixed pirate raids proceeding from the North Sea coast immediately upon the northeastern limits of the Empire: the mouths of the Ems, the Weser, and the Elbe, and the shores of the Bight of Heligoland—that is, the Frisian western shores of what we call today Schleswig-Holstein.

The story that they overran Britain, drove out the original British inhabitants, and resettled the island, is nonsense; but what is true is that in the general breakdown of Roman administration, local heads of pirate bands took over local government over a narrow belt along the eastern and southeastern shores of what is today called

England. It was this group that was called by the general term "Saxon," and that raided the shores around Calais and Boulogne and southeastern Belgium as well as the island of Britain. It is interesting to note that one portion of the pirate groups were called "Angles" or "Engles," from which we get our modern words "English" and "England." The word presumably arose from the Latin word "angulus," which meant, among other things, a Bight, and would apply to the Bight of Heligoland. As so often happens, the savages took on their name from an appellation which an alien civilization had given them.

These preliminary attacks from oversea by pirates began very early, indeed they began long before the breakdown of Roman administration. They were already recurrent and fairly severe in the century before Constantine, and kept on getting worse and worse up to the year 500. They had the effect of cutting off what was still Christian England from the Continent and therefore causing society in the island to sink yet lower.

When the energy of these first pirate raids that crossed the North Sea was exhausted, the Pope of the day sent out misisonaries to convert the eastern belt of Britain where civilization had largely disappeared with the Christian religion upon which it depended. The Pope's emissary, St. Augustine, and his companions, came over from fully Christian France just before the year 600, and before the end of the following century they had established the Mass, and writing, and proper building, and civilization in general throughout that eastern belt of Britain which the raids had half ruined. To this success of theirs attached a very interesting consequence: they had sought, for the conversion of the barbaric eastern strip of Britain, the aid of the still Christian though impoverished and degraded, west of Britain; but the Christian Kinglets and

Bishops of the West refused to help the Italian missionaries, perhaps because they feared foreign domination. The result was that the Church, which was then altogether the most important, indeed the only, large organization of the day, with all the strength that modern Capitalism has in half-developed countries of our own time, threw its weight in favor of the little chieftains on the east coast of Britain against those of the west.

Ireland was already Catholic through a process of conversion which had begun from the Christian side of Britain two hundred years before. Irish missionaries did, indeed, agree to help the Roman effort at converting the barbarized strip of Eastern Britain, but they did not agree with the general customs of the Latin Church, especially in the observance of Easter. In a council held in Whitby on the coast of Yorkshire, the arguments for conformity with the Roman usages prevailed, and the full unity of the Church in Britain along with the Latin or Western Church on the Continent was ultimately accomplished.

It was the language, therefore, of the petty courts in York and in Bamburgh on the coast of the North Sea and in Norfolk and in Suffolk, Essex and Kent, that was spread through the missionary schools and through the Church's effort, as civilization was recovered westward throughout the island. That is why England and its expansion speaks English today, a language half Latin and half Teutonic, instead of speaking a language half Latin and half Celtic.

With Britain thus recovered for the imperiled Catholic civilization of Western Europe, there was a lull lasting about a hundred years so far as pirate expeditions overseas against Christendom were concerned. The heavy fighting of the day was done against the savage Germans of the continent and the Mongols coming up the Danube valley and the plains to the north of it. That was the moment when western civilization was gathered into one state under the chief ruler of Gaul, King Charles, who was crowned Emperor of the West at Rome in the year 800 and is called in history Charlemagne.

There were indeed bad raids by Scandinavian pirates, though no actual invasion until after Charlemagne's death in 814. But during the succeeding century and more, the pirate attacks increased in vigor and began to make settlements in the island of Britain and on the coasts of northern and western France and on the banks of the rivers in both countries. The second wave of murderous piracy came from the southern part of what we call today Norway and Sweden and the peninsula of Denmark. The pirates were known in England as Danes and on the continent as the men from the north, or Northmen, which was contracted into Normans. As with the first wave of pirates, they were not numerous—a boat held on the average not more than fifty fighting men and all their vessels combined came only to a few.*

These pirates who came across and down the North Sea raided England continuously and northern France as well. In northern France their chief, a certain Rollo, was accepted by the Christian Empire, as so many of his kind had been in the past. He was allowed to take over local government, his fighting men intermarried with the landowning families of the lower Seine, and a new local chief took over the government of the province then called the Second Lyonnese, but now called Normandy. He ruled from Rouen, and, of course, the few thousand Scandi-

---

* The largest single attack was that made on the new Christian settlements at the mouth of the Elbe, where Charlemagne had forced the German savages to become civilized, baptizing them under pain of death. It is to be remembered that this great attack on Hamburg failed. It comprised 600 vessels, so altogether there could not have been more than 3000 fighting men.

navians soon melted into the general Gallo-Roman population, spoke the same language, northern French, the ancestor of modern French. In other words, these few invaders were rapidly digested into the mass of civilization.*

The pirate invasions against Gaul thus ceased a long lifetime before the year 1000. But they went on against England much longer, and England as a province of Roman civilization was almost overwhelmed by their destructive efforts. But the Christian people of the island rallied under Alfred and his successors and even while they suffered the blows of the pirates, succeeded in converting them and half civilizing them. At last, just after the year 1000, the raids of the Scandinavian pirate kings against England turned into a dynastic movement. They were already half Christian at home as well as abroad. But they kept up a foreign pressure against the English, which did not end until the Dukes of Normany with a large French-speaking army of their own and many mercenaries from northern France came over and founded medieval England in 1066.

One may say that on this sector, the northeastern sector, the siege of Christendom was definitely raised. So it was on the mid-eastern sector. Pagan Mongol raids of light cavalry, even more murderous and destructive than the Scandinavian pirates, were checked by the now Christian Germans of the Rhine and the lower Elbe and the upper Danube. The furthest outpost of the Mongol raiders had gone as far west as the river Saone in France. They reached the town of Tournus, today on

---

* We often come across in modern books written in the English tongue the term "Norman French." That term is merely a piece of anti-Catholic propaganda. There never was any such tongue as Norman French. The Duke of Normandy and his nobles and squires and all the people spoke the same French as was spoken from the Loire to the Channel and from the Ardennes to the boundaries of Breton speech.

the main railway line between Paris and Marseilles. But long before the year 1000 they had ebbed back to the plains of Hungary, a country which takes its name and its language from Mongol sources.

So much for the pagan raiders from Scandinavia. Further east were the Slavonic raiders.

The Slavs came down in confused, uncoördinated tribes called by various names, and thrusting from the great northern plains down into the Balkans. There they harried the Greek Empire, but Constantinople always stood up to them and retained fluctuating power in the highlands of what we call today Jugoslavia and Bulgaria. The Slavs also were converted, but converted, of course, by Greek missionaries, who gave them the Greek liturgy, that is, the Greek Mass, and the Greek alphabet. There also was among them a Slavonic liturgy, and the Mass is still said in old Slavonic in part of the Balkans and in old Russia.

In this mass conversion of the Slavs by Byzantine missionaries, one exception arose: that northern group of them who later were called Poles, received the western influence coming from Germany; they dropped the Greek liturgy and adopted the Latin. When the separation between the Eastern and Western Churches became more distinct, the Poles represented the Western or Latin civilization in the Slav world.

We have seen that the siege of Christendom on its southeastern sector, that is, from Asia Minor to Syria, and Egypt, was of quite a different character from what it was in the north and center of Europe. We have seen that in the north and center it was an attack of savages by sea and land, without culture, letters or any system of government worthy of the name. The pressure was very heavy and lasted a long time, but the siege was raised, the attack was beaten back and Christendom itself triumphantly advanced over the populations and into the territories which had been those of the enemy.

In the south however the siege of Christendom by its enemies was successful. It was never raised.

It was undertaken at first by very small numbers but under the inspiration of a religious zeal—Mahommedanism—and *with the exceptional opportunity they had,* the attackers took over that part of Christendom, the Greek part, which they attacked. They took over its culture, its arts, its building, its general social structure, its land survey (on which the taxes were based) and all the rest of it. But the attackers imposed their new heresy which gradually became a new religion and which held power over government and society wherever the attack broke our eastern siege-line and occupied Christian territory. The result was a complete transformation of society which rapidly grew into a violent contrast between the Orient and Europe. Mahommedanism planted itself firmly not only throughout Syria but all along North Africa and even into Spain, and overflowed vigorously into Asia eastward.

The opportunity for the attack on this sector was exceptional. The high Greek civilization centralized in Constantinople and its wealthy Imperial Court defended by a highly trained professional army, possessing great revenues as well, might have seemed superficially far better able to resist assaults than was Western Europe, with its conditions already half barbaric through the long material decline, with its lack of regular armies and its division into half-independent local groups. But as a fact the blow delivered against the Greeks, the Christendom of the southeast, cracked the shell and had more immediate and more profound consequences than the mere raids of the east and north.

The opportunities given for the attack from the southeast were fourfold. First, debt was universal (as it is with us today); secondly, taxes were very heavy; thirdly, a large proportion of the population were slaves; fourthly, both law and theology, that is, both social practice and religious rules had become more complex than the masses could follow.

A new reforming enthusiasm invading the Empire could take advantage of all these four weaknesses: it could promise the indebted farmer, the indebted municipal authority, the wiping out of their debts; it could promise the heavily burdened small taxpayer relief from his burden; it could promise freedom to the slave and it could promise a simple—a far too simple—new set of rules for Society and new set of practices in religion. It was this fourth appeal, the appeal to simplification, especially to simplification of religion and morals, which had the greatest force. It worked in Syria and Egypt at that moment just as it worked nine centuries later in the West during the Reformation.

This intense enthusiasm for reform arose almost wholly from the personal driving-power of one man, an Arab camel driver called Mahommed. Like all the Arabs around him in that desert region outside the jurisdiction of the Christian Empire under Constantinople, he was born a pagan. But having wandered far afield he was deeply stirred by the religious systems, Christian and Jewish, which he came across in the civilized world. Certain main tenets appealed to him intensely; he summed them up in a body of doctrine which remained his own. He became passionately attached to the idea of the personal omnipotent God, the creator of all things, to His justice and His mercy, to the corresponding double fate of mankind, Heaven or Hell, to the reality of the world of good, as well as of evil, spirits, to the resurrection and immortality of human beings. All this group of simple fundamental Catholic doctrine he not only accepted but was permeated by. He was struck with awe at the contemplation of Christ and regarded Our Lord as the very first of moral teachers and renovators of the spiritual life. And he paid deep veneration to Our Lady.

But a priesthood, (which to his mind was a useless social complexity) the whole sacramental system which went with a priesthood, and that central essential pillar of Christendom, the Mass, he rejected altogether. He also rejected baptism, retaining or accepting circumcision not only as a Jewish rite but as common among his own people. He allowed a relaxed sexual morality, concubinage and a plurality of legitimate wives, as also very easy divorce.

We must presume that this powerful zealot was sincere, that he felt vouchsafed within him a divine revelation and a mission to spread it by his burning enthusiasm. He felt himself to be in the line of the greater prophets, the last and the greatest of them all. There may have been an element of the charlatan and deceiver about him, as his enemies believed and as many modern scholars and historians still incline to believe in part. But for the main, for his right to his mission and his claim to be the supreme prophet of God we must believe that he was sincere. At any rate the band of men whom he convinced and gathered around him, established the new heresy; (for it was essentially a Christian heresy at first, though arising just outside the boundaries of Christendom) fiercely propagated it by arms—a spirit which strongly appealed to the Arab temper. The seed took vigorous root and shortly after Mahommed's death the band of mounted warriors burning to spread the intense doctrine he had framed for them, burst through the confines of civilization where the desert meets the cultivated land east of Jordan.

Their success was amazing. They took Damascus which

is the key of all the Near East and in the valley of the Yarmuk they defeated the regular Christian Byzantine Army sent against them, though it vastly exceeded them in numbers. They swept over Syria and Mesopotamia, organizing their new power everywhere, offering freedom to the slaves and the debtors, and relief to the taxpayer wherever these would accept the religion of Mahommed. And the simplicity of that religion powerfully aided their effort. Men desiring freedom from thraldom and from debt and from the weight of the imposts, joined them everywhere in great numbers. There arose a governing Mahommedan nucleus which alone had armed power and which vastly exceeded in numbers the original cavalcade that had set out from the Arabian sands. The great majority of the population remained, of course, still attached more or less directly to their Catholic traditions or those of their local heresies; their practices of liturgy were tolerated by the new masters, but they no longer had any political power and all the armament was in the hands of those who were now their superiors.

This system of Mahommedan government over great regions of Christian culture spread with amazing rapidity; it swamped Egypt, using henceforward the revenues of its great wealth in the Delta and the Valley of the Nile. It passed over and dominated the Greek-speaking, Punic-speaking and Latin-speaking cities of the North African shore lying between the Mediterranean and the desert. The triumphant invasion did not cease even when it had reached the Atlantic, it crossed the Straits of Gibraltar, it overran the Spanish peninsula, it crossed the Pyrenees and attempted to do to Western Christendom what it had done to Eastern.

The great wave broke when its crest had reached the center of Gaul. In a vast battle fought halfway between Tours and Poitiers the Christians under the leadership of one of the wealthiest and greatest of the Gallo-Roman families mixed with German blood—the family from which Charlemagne was to come—threw back the invasion to the Pyrenees. But beyond the Pyrenees this strange new Arabian thing, though but a small minority in numbers, was supreme over government and arms.

The pace of that expansion was so astonishing as to be still claimed by the Mahommedans as miraculous and as the proof of their prophet's divine mission. The original battle of the Yarmuk when the first Byzantine army had been astonished into sudden defeat at the hands of quite unexpected foes, took place in 634. The battle between Tours and Poitiers in the heart of France was fought in 732. Not a hundred years, little more than one long lifetime, had sufficed for this prodigious expansion.

The siege of Christendom on this side, to the southeast and the south, had indeed succeeded: save in Spain itself, it was never raised. On the contrary the pressure against Christendom in the east was to remain continuous and at last to threaten all our civilization again. The Mahommedan was at the gates of Vienna less than a hundred years before the Declaration of Independence. Had he taken Vienna he would have reached the Rhine.

Such had been what I have called "The Siege of Christendom"; the 8th, 9th, and 10th centuries to which more properly than any other—but especially to the 9th and the greater part of the 10th—may be applied to the term "Dark Ages." These generations of peril, continual fighting against external enemies and uninterrupted struggle had upon our mortally threatened civilization an effect of the greatest import for our future. That effect may be called by metaphor "annealing." The pressure and heat of the struggle confirmed Christian Europe in the mould wherein it had been cast. It consolidated our society, and gave it that form which was to prove vigorous and enduring and provide the "taking-off place" for the great expansion of the true Middle Ages about to follow.

What had the social structure of Christendom become during those three centuries of unceasing defensive combat? In the first place the internal social structure of the West had consolidated and taken on a new and enduring character.

Slavery properly so-called, the buying and selling of men and women and exploitation of their labor by mere force had ceased to be the foundation of Society. In its place there had developed a state of affairs in which the former slave had become the *Serf*. The descendants of the slaves were no longer working at the arbitrary will of masters here and there upon the great landed estates; they were fixed in village communities over which the former owner remained master, but a master with rights now strictly limited by custom.

The serf was the halfway house between the Slave of pagan antiquity and the Free Peasant of later Christian centuries. The great bulk—at least nine-tenths—of Christian men in the West were agricultural. In the German-speaking belt of the Rhine valley and its margin immediately to the east, in the equally German districts of the upper Danube, in Gaul (or France), Britain, Italy and that part of Spain towards the north which had been recovered by Christian armies from the Mahommedan, at least nine families out of ten were tilling the earth, and of these some large majority, perhaps two-thirds, were serfs attaching to the soil, still compelled to work as their slave forefathers had been, for other men, acting as bondsmen to lords, but their work strictly limited by what had become immemorial custom. So many days a week the serf had to give to the lord's own farmland, but the rest of his time was his own. Of the produce of his own land, so much he had to give in dues to the Church and the local lord; but the rest was, in practice, at his own disposal. In other words, the isolation of the villages during the long wars of the siege of Christendom, the very fact that intercommunication had become difficult, produced a self-sufficing and fully organized village community.

But there was one force which had thus already half emancipated the old slave class, and given it gradually throughout the centuries the higher position it had achieved: and that force was the religion common to lord and slave alike. All men felt themselves under the challenge of the outer barbarism, to be of one Christian stuff: one united and superior civilization which had to remain alive through its own energy.

It has often been said that the gradual evolution during the Dark Ages, of the slave into the half-free serf, his progress on the way to becoming a free peasant, was a blind economic development. It was the fashion of the 19th century to talk this way, because, fundamentally, the 19th century error was materialism, and that materialistic philosophy led men into bad history.

There was no economic reason for the decay of the old servitude and the increase of personal position and freedom in what had become the mass of the unfree. It is Mind which determines the change of Society, and it was because the mind at work was a Catholic mind that the slave became a serf and was on his way to becoming a peasant and a fully free man—a man free economically as well as politically. The whole spirit of the Church was for small property, and that spirit was slowly, instinctively, working for the establishment of small property throughout Christendom. It was small property subject to servitudes, paying heavy dues to others; but it was small property just the same, and it had struck permanent root.

Corresponding to this development in the agricultural world which was nine-tenths of that society, was the development in the world of craftsmen and artisans and the life of the towns. There the Guild, binding groups of craftsmen together, limiting competition, fostering a corporate life, mirrored the arrangements of the villages. The rules of the Christian Guild, and still more of its spirit, forbade the accumulation of wealth in a few hands —the eating up of the small man by the great. The work of the apprentice was indeed subject to exploitation by his master, but the apprentice became of right a master in his turn, and the carpenters, masons, clothiers and the rest at the end of the Dark Ages were thus organized throughout Christendom in self-sufficing and self-govern-ing bodies, bound together by traditions not yet explicit as they later became, not yet generally codified as they later were, but of living force to preserve the proper livelihood of Christian men.

Such was the effect of that process of "annealing" upon the agricultural mass of Society, which included, be it remembered, not only the descendants of the old slaves but the smaller free farmers as well. And such was its effect upon the craftsmen of the towns, and all those of the common people who lived otherwise than by tillage. There remained patches of actual servile condition; there were cases still of men bought and sold, but they were highly exceptional and the exceptions soon died out.

The dues paid and the services rendered according to a fixed custom by the village communities to their lords supported those village lords in a class of their own; and sundry other dues also supported another caste of Society —the clergy. The mass of feudal lords were small lords of one village or two or three at the most; and an inter-mediate class had acquired through marriage and in-heritance groups of villages, rendering them more wealthy, while well above these were the few great regional fortunes which took dues from and governed whole districts.

These districts again were grouped loosely and by personal ties into kingships. The feudal class of lords, from the small village lord to the largest owners, had become now for generations since the siege of Christendom, not ony politically the governing class but the fighting class of Society. Theirs was the business of defense and of expanding the territory of Christendom.

The society of Christendom undergoing its slow transformation during the pressure of this great "siege," as I have called it, developed three characteristics which stamped themselves upon the European nature till long after the siege-conditions had disappeared. They were stamped upon the form of Europe till the Renaissance and beyond. We still have relics of them today.

The first of these characteristics was a profound underlying sense of Christian unity and particularly of Western Christian unity: the unity of all those bound together by the Latin Mass and by the Western Patriarchy, at the head of which was the Bishop of Rome, the Pope.

The military power of the pagan Roman Empire had never achieved a moral unity of this kind. It had imposed a political unity and a certain pride in citizenship, but it did not provide that spiritual bond without which a society can never be really one. Today we think in terms of independent states and races. Some are even so superficial as to think mainly in terms of common language. But the prime factor of unity in any society, large or small, is for all the members of that society to hold the same philosophy, to put human affairs in the same order of importance, and to be agreed on the prime matters of right and wrong and of public worship.

The second characteristic was the development of a noble caste. There arose in men's minds the conception of "blood": a sort of mystical distinction between one kind of descent and another.

Men have debated the origins of this strong feeling and usually come to erroneous conclusions thereon. There has, of course, been the non-rational or mystical conception of caste in any number of human societies from the remotest past. Sometimes these seem to have arisen from conquest. At some date before recorded history a religious feeling led to the worship of a particular clan or section of the community. There were even among the outer Germans, who had on this, as in most things, ideas less precise than their neighbors to the south and west, feelings that this or that family was sacred, so that the chieftain of the tribe could be taken from that family and no other. Such an arrangement can be found in others of the half-civilized outer fringe beyond the strict boundaries of the old Roman Empire. But the feeling of the rank which developed in Christendom during the Dark Ages and took very firm root had quite another source. It proceeded from leadership in war. The leaders of the loosely organized Christian forces which withstood the pressure of anti-Christian barbarism on the north and Mahommedan hatred on the south, were in the main the descendants of the old Roman landowners, the possessors of the great country estates tilled by their slaves. These were the one wealthy and dominating class at the end of the direct government of the West, from Rome. They became the natural chiefs of the bands drawn from their freemen and armed at their expense. These bands were levied either for local defense against the pagan invasions or for private war or for the formation of some great hosts when such an agglomeration was necessary to meet a particular severe strain. Alfred of England, to give one example out of hundreds, levied a considerable force of this kind from the southern counties when he set out to prevent this part of Britain being wholly laid waste by the pagan pirates. He summoned, in the words of the contemporary record, the "men of Dorset and the men of Wiltshire, but the men of Hampshire had fled oversea." This does not mean, of course, that Alfred summoned all the inhabitants of the counties near his standard when he had set it up in Penselwood, where Dorset and Somerset meet. It means that he summoned what we call today the squires, the great landowners, each followed by his small band of armed men.

The fighting class thus formed, grew, as the siege of Christendom proceeded, to regard itself as something special among them. It was not only the richest class but it did the most arduous and perilous work for the community, and there arose the conception of the armed mounted man as a being apart, superior of his nature to the rest of lay mankind. He was the "noblesse," a man of race (which is the original meaning of the English word "gentleman").

No doubt this half-religious feeling, this distinction of "blood," this separation of a leading class apart from the mass of the community, was reinforced by ancestral memories. The Gauls had a very strong feeling of the distinction between a nobility and the mass of the clan, as they also had a very strong feeling of the distinction between the man consecrated to religion and the layman. Gaul remained the center and main area of Christendom during the Great Siege. The Gallic spirit and the Gallic race gave its tone to the society of all Western Europe in those days when Western Europe was only kept alive by the perpetual movements of armed forces mainly recruited from the area of what is today called France. But whatever other elements entered into the business, the main element was this: the prestige of the principal fighting men. That fighting class received dues from the villages, of which its families were the lords, and organized itself in a rough hierarchy, which we call feudalism.

That hierarchy was, as to its steps or ranks, principally distinguished by income. Your lord of one manor or village might receive in dues what we should call today $5000. to $10,000. in a year. His wealthier neighbor, receiving dues from several manors, would be on the scale of anything from $5000. to $100,000. a year. Then above these would come the great overlords, each of whom not only possessed many villages himself, making him richer than anyone else in the district, but also rights over public land which had formerly been the Treasury Land of the Roman emperors—all that lay outside the manorial system. The very highest of these great landed men, those who stood at the summit of the feudal pyramid, became in local power indistinguishable from monarchs. A Count of Flanders or of Anjou or a Duke of Normandy was supreme in his own district. He would owe feudal homage to the King of France. He would admit the titular sovereignty of the King of France, and on very rare occasions when the King of France (himself chief feudal lord of the district around Paris) summoned a quasi-national effort under arms, the local ruler of Anjou and Normandy and the rest, was appealed to, but he would only come of his own free will.

The third characteristic which the siege of Christendom produced during that annealment of Christian men was the almost imperceptibly slow emancipation of those who had been in the old pagan time, and remained for many generations afterwards, slaves. Of this gradual transformation whereby the slave who in the first centuries of Christian Europe could be bought and sold like any other chattel, turned later into the completely free peasant of modern times, there has already been mention. What we have to note here is the profundity of the social revolution thus effected. The old terms were used continuously for centuries. The very word "serf" which we write today with the special object of distinguishing a man who was *not* a slave, only constrained to certain fixed labor, possessed of property and of hereditary rights, and engaged for the most part upon labor the fruits of which he himself enjoyed, is merely the Latin word for *slave,* given a later form.

Nothing intentional was at work, no direct and explicit laws or edicts produced any one step in this very slow instinctive development of the pagan slave into the Christian peasant—a matter of a thousand years. Nevertheless, the real agency at work is plain enough when one sees the thing on its largest lines. That agency was the religion which all men held in common, of whatever rank, whatever poverty, or whatever wealth. It had in the beginning of the process become more and more impossible morally to "buy and sell Christian men." The separation of families under the system of slavery was not consonant with the ethic to which converted Europe was bound. It was this, much more than any economic development, which effected the great change, and of all the changes which the Catholic spirit of Europe wrought during the pressure of the Great Siege, this was the most enduring.

It has so thoroughly recast the whole political and social conscience of Western European man that he has forgotten his servile origins. He is penetrated with the conception of citizenship spread over the whole community. All his modern experiments take it for granted, from the sanest to the most extravagant.

But let this be noted: Even as we gradually transformed ourselves from slaves into freemen under the influence of the Catholic Faith, so in the loss of it we are beginning to tread the road downward again. With the decay of religion, that which none of the reformers dream of (as yet), but which is apparent by implication in all they do, the Servile State, Society based upon and marked with the stamp of slavery is returning.

Let it be further noted that the great lapse of time of this "siege," during which Christendom in its isolation and peril and suffering and pressure from without, had ceased to develop its already decayed material civilization, had lost the conception of universal codified law and lived by custom and tradition; produced by its very duration a certain spirit the opposite of that connected with our modern activities—but also with our modern unrest and danger of disruption.

It produced a spirit of Status, individuals and the classes of Society being bound one to another not by terminable contract as they are today, but by the conception that every man had his place and fixed duties which he had inherited and could hand on to his descendants. The serf paying his dues of labor and produce, the small free man who lived side by side with him in the village and was also bound by custom to certain dues, the lords of villages receiving their feudal incomes, the overlords above them, the craftsmen in the towns, all these took for granted each his position in an organized society which called from each man certain activities, but guaranteed subsistence and the family.

There was exploitation; there was the institution of one man working for the profit of another; but it worked by fixed rules and inheritance, not by competition; the livelihood of those working was not in jeopardy, the revenues paid to superiors in that feudal society were known and fixed, the class distinctions consecrated by the immense length of time through which they had grown and by the fixity of the succession from generation to generation.

Christian society had become static—but static also means stable. It had become an organized thing the rules of whose life would remain a strong framework preserving the character of the whole and its shape through the coming expansion of energy and knowledge.

On account of this fixity, of this mass of traditional custom taken for granted in all men's minds, but most of all on account of the universal accepted religion with its ubiquitous liturgy and philosophy explaining the nature and spiritual doom or beatitude of man, his immortality and his relation to the Divine—as to all these things at the end of the Dark Ages, the soul of Europe stood upon solid ground.

We are about to see it passing into a new phase of intense activity when it flowered into the true Middle Ages and established what was perhaps the highest point in the history of our race.

(b) THE HIGH MIDDLE AGES

We are discussing a civilization the highest and the best of which history has any record; the civilization of Christendom. We have followed its strange birth, its rapid growth and strong organization, its triumph over the whole world, that is, its capture of the pagan Græco-Roman Empire in which are rooted all the traditions of our culture and from which we all descend. For Christendom indeed, is no more than "the Empire baptized"— but that "no more" is of such prodigious magnitude that it is beyond all hyperbole. The conversion of the Empire and the consequences thereof form the capital event in the history of the world.

Since we are so discussing a particular civilization, how it was formed and established by its united philosophy of religion, and since we must regard that civilization as the supreme thing it was and is, we approach the climax of its manifestation with a certain awe. That climax followed on the great siege which Christendom had stood during the Dark Ages and had so successfully beaten off so far as the West, at least, was concerned. In the first generation of the 11th century—say about 1020 to 1030—when, the siege having been successfully raised, Christendom began to go forward sure of itself, burgeoning and putting forth its fresh powers, then was the beginning of the period during which our people, our culture were most themselves, when the effect of the religion which made us was wholly mature, complete, and victorious. It may best be called "The High Middle Ages" and it covers the great 300 years of the 11th, 12th, and 13th centuries, that is until after the date 1300.

The term "Middle Ages" like the term "Dark Ages" has been used very loosely and generally. We do well, therefore, to define our terms. We have already defined what may properly be called the Dark Ages—the time during which Christendom was constantly under peril and pressure, when so much of material civilization was lost and when at the cost of continual and mortal struggle our fathers survived the attack of barbarism. This succeeding and cross-phase in our story, the Middle Ages, may be said to last until the Renaissance, the fall of Constantinople, the revolution in the arts and general culture, and the disaster of the Reformation, when what had so long been our united common heritage was broken and divided.

The whole of such a period would cover 500 years, somewhat after the year 1000 and somewhat after the year 1500, and it is, indeed, to this long stretch of 500 years that the term "Middle Ages," is commonly applied. But we understand the thing much better if we distinguish between the earlier and the later part.

The first 300 years, which, I say, may properly be called the true Middle Ages, because the virtues of medieval civilization were at their highest and its characteristics at their strongest and best, came to an end with the early 14th century. The remaining 200 years, from the beginning at least of the Great Schism until the wild revolt of Luther and the anti-Catholic edifice of Calvin, have a very different savor. The mass of the 14th and all the 15th century is a period in which external civilization is rising, but in which the soul of Christendom progressively suffers. With that lamentable spiritual decline we will deal next. Here we are engaged upon the flowering of Christendom, the summit reaching up to the full development of the 13th century: 1200 A.D.-1300 A.D.

Let not any man's admiration of this, the chief achievement of our race, be lessened or warped by the inevitable contrast between the present and the past. Manifestly, one period will have advantages which another period lacks, the better period will be less fortunate in many things than the worse period which succeeds it. The elements of a culture are always in process of change. But those who cannot feel the call of the true Middle Ages and their correspondence to all that is strongest in our blood, those who complain that they lack amenities we now possess, forgetting how much we have also lost, have a poor comprehension of history. Were the most devoted modern man and the greatest admirer of that time to find himself put down suddenly upon the peak of the true Middle Ages, say the year 1270, he would miss very much that is necessary to him. He would be in an atmosphere which, however congenial to him, would be foreign. But it is the part of wisdom to mark the difference in quality between what has been lost and what has been gained. An example in one sentence may suffice: *"There were no potatoes, but then, also, there were no suicides."*

We start then with that first generation of the 11th century. The Scandinavian pirates who had attacked us over the North Sea had been converted. Much of their barbarism remains, but they will never more threaten destruction. They have become part of our culture.

The hordes, a mixture of ill defined types, (many of them Slavonic), who had attacked the center of Europe, were defeated and tamed, even the Mongols. Hungary itself where the Mongols had fixed themselves was already baptized, and the West was secure. The Mahommedan attack, indeed, had succeeded; it had captured and was holding all that part of Christendom which had lain along the southern and eastern Mediterranean, and later it was to go further still. But in the West, at any rate, we had begun to press back even that formidable foe. For in northern Spain the reconquest of the peninsula had begun. Navarre had proved itself in policy worthy of independence, Aragon was founded, the beginnings of Castile had appeared. "The March of the Ebro," the Catalan forework, challenging the Mahommedan power at Saragossa, was permanently held.

The advance had begun.

It is well to take the great period by its three centuries: A.D. 1000 to A.D. 1300. It is not, of course, exactly divided by each term of 100 years, but falls into three main divisions which, with some overlap, do roughly correspond to such an arrangement.

There is, first, what may be called the 11th century, from this first generation, say 1020-1030 to the opening generation beyond the year 1100, which saw the initial success of the first great Crusade.

The next period, also about 100 years, the 12th century, which overlaps into the 13th, gives us the establishment of nearly all our great institutions, the Parliaments, the

Universities and the rest. It is the moment of the Plantagenet power in England and its rival, the newly strengthened kingdom of France. It gives us also the characteristic architecture of the Middle Ages, generally called the Gothic—the pointed arch, the type of the great remaining cathedrals of the period.

The greatest century of all follows, the 13th, which we may take from the Battle of Muret, the great Christian victory in Spain of Navas, and, a minor matter, the date of Magna Charta* in England. This century is the century of the great medieval characters—of the Friars—that is of St. Dominic and St. Francis—the summit of medieval philosophy (the work of St. Thomas Aquinas) the summit of medieval literature, for, though the Divine Comedy appears just on and after A.D. 1300, the supreme poet was the last generation of that time. (A.D. 1265-A.D. 1321).

To begin with the 11th century.

We were still emerging from darkness. There was still much that was half barbaric about our society. Look at the imperfect sculpture, the crude ornament which still is attempted on the strong capitals of the Romanesque, or read the splendid but unpolished epic, *The Song of Roland,* or mark the simplicity of strategy and tactics. The first sign of the coming change was the further centralization of power in the Church and the beginning of a new challenge to the encroachments of lay government. The Church is not only centralized, but its discipline of celibacy is strengthened and perfected. The Papacy, which in the West was not only the symbol but, in a fashion, the cause of unity, took on such new vigor that its enemies have called it a change in character. This it

---

* "Magna *Ch*arta" is the age-long, traditional English name of this document, which, though corrupt should be retained. The more correct "Magna *C*arta" is a modern innovation.

was not. It was a strengthening and development without which we should never have had the high civilization that was to follow. The spirit that presided over this change was that of the great Benedictine abbey, the abbey of Cluny. The Cluniac spirit informed the whole, and Cluny sent out that very great man with whose name the separation of the Papacy and the Church in general from lay control will always be bound up—Hildebrand of Tuscany. Here a caution must be issued against the popular anti-Catholic myth appearing in a host of textbooks, most typically, perhaps, in the monograph of Bryce on the Holy Roman Empire. There was propagated a myth that the Saxon Emperors invading Italy from the Northern Germanies originated the regeneration of Papal power.

They did nothing of the kind. It is true that, at the end of the Dark Ages, the institution of the Papacy had gone through a bad period; great families had captured it to their own profit; immature members of them and unworthy members had occupied the central see, and reform was due. But the reform of the Saxon Emperors had not for its main motive, reform; it had for its main motive the thrusting back of Byzantine power.

The Emperor of Constantinople, who had never really accepted the imperial title in the West, did what he could to maintain his hold upon Italy and still dreamed of being the civil head of all Christendom, with Popes to be in the long run as subservient to him as were the metropolitans of New Rome on the Bosphorus. It was against this influence that the Saxon Emperors moved, and, had they succeeded, they would have made the Papacy a German thing. The successor of St. Peter would have been nominated by the German Kings, and the lay power would have reasserted itself more than ever. From that the great Hildebrandine Reform saved us. The thing was not done without violent struggle. Hildebrand himself, when, from being the chief adviser of the Papacy, he had become Pope (St. Gregory VII), died under the impression of defeat. Everyone knows the famous cry, "I have loved justice and hated iniquity, and therefore I die in exile." In reality, St. Gregory had won, for there came in to support the newly invigorated Papacy the strength of the Normans.

The coming of the Norman state and soldiery is a peculiar episode standing at the origins of the true Middle Ages and coloring them for three generations. Having had this strong effect, the special Norman character disappears.

What made this new "Norman energy," the second characteristic of the opening 11th century and the founding of the true Middle Ages? Why, having arisen, did it disappear so soon?

It is in full activity before the middle of the century when the Duke of Normandy, Robert the Devil, left his throne to that illegitimate son of his who was to become so famous, William of Falaise. It was at its height when this same William of Falaise established his claim to the throne of England at Hastings, continued under Bohemond during all the first Crusade, then almost suddenly in the next lifetime it is gone.

The question of how this strange thing arose, why it was so limited in time, and the rest, certainly cannot be fully answered. One suggestion is that, just as a small proportion of carbon turns iron into steel, so some small proportion of Scandinavian northern blood mixing with the Gallo-Romans of the Second Lyonnese accounts for the short-lived Norman race and power. It may be so. The Second Lyonnese had been given by the Emperor to the command of a Scandinavian pirate force which had harried it a century before during the Dark Ages, and the

chief fighting men of that Scandinavian body had intermarried with the lords of the Cotentin and the lower
Seine valley. That admixture of blood may have had in
the long run some effect.

At any rate, the thing happened. Men filled with the
spirit of adventure, singularly constructive, astute or-
ganizers as well as great soldiers, came from Normandy
for three generations. A small body of such sprung from
a family of middle nobles near the western coast of the
Norman province set out to try their fortunes in South
Italy, which had been harried by the Mohammedan and
which the Byzantines, who claimed to be the rightful
government there, ill defended. These adventurers hired
themselves out and took the risks of battle against the
Mohammedans, as also against the dwindling Byzantine
power. They married the local heiresses; they recruited
larger and larger forces from the local south Italian and
Sicilian inhabitants as their successes increased; they joined
forces with the Papacy, supporting it against the Germans
and against the Greeks. They ended by holding from the
Papacy as feudal kings Sicilian Naples and what had been
the Greek cities and territories in Italy south of the Papal
States. Their government became a model of precision,
accuracy, and centralized power, and it was a younger
son of that same now royal family who became the chief
figure of the First Crusade.

While this vigorous thrust was going forward, the
Norman occupation of power in South Italy and Sicily and
the later establishment of a Norman dynasty in England,
the local monarchies, long existing in name, were beginning to gather power. Those which sprang from the valleys of the Pyrenees and the unconquered fringe of northern Spain grew powerful through gradual success over
the Mahommedans. Provence exhibited a separate life,
and the House that was the feudal head of all the great

French districts, normally superior to the local rulers of Normandy and Brittany, Flanders, Aquitaine and the rest, the House of Paris (it had long borne title "Kings of France") gave signs of the strength which it was to increase so greatly in the next generation.

Yet another mark of the new energy was what has been finely called "The Awakening of the Great Curiosity." (The phrase is Michelet's.) It was an intellectual movement not without peril. It engendered the first of the great heresies which were to endanger our reinvigorated Christendom, but it was a mark of superabundant life. For the first time since the disastrous Mahommedan enthusiasm, the mysteries of religion were attacked, but this time from within.

The central rite, the vital liturgy of Christendom, the pivot, as it were, of all the faith in action, the Blessed Sacrament, was challenged. The challenge is associated with the name of a cleric of north France, a Canon of Tours, one Berengarius. He first began to rationalize that which Mahommed in his violent simplification of religion had abandoned altogether. The new heretical effort did not abandon the Real Presence, but it attempted to modify the doctrine on rationalist lines.

The great and successful opponent of Berengarius, Lanfranc, the mighty Italian who was the right hand of William the Conqueror in England, was Archbishop of Canterbury and the champion of the Sacrament of the Altar. It was from this controversy that arose, it would seem, what has become one of the characteristic gestures in the liturgy of the Western Church and of the Latin Mass: the Elevation. Lanfranc originated a habit of pausing for a moment over the Host immediately after Consecration and raising it slightly before his face to adore it. From this, it is believed, the Elevation in its later form grew.

At the very end of this first division of our period, the 11th century, came the most famous manifestation of its young, exuberant power, the Crusades. A new wave of Turkish barbarism had made itself master of the Near East, including the holy places. Pilgrimage thither, which, in spite of the Mahommedan power, had been continuous, grew difficult. A great Turkish victory had imperiled the Greek Christian culture and come to the gates of Constantinople itself. The reaction to all this had been the outpouring of crusaders by the hundred thousand at the call of the Pope, Urban II, who carried on the tradition and the work of Hildebrand. Several armies on the scale of 80,000 men each, were gathering. When the final strength was reached, something like a third of a million men accompanied by perhaps as many again of half-armed or unarmed pilgrims, crossed the ruined and deserted land of Asia Minor, took Antioch, pressed through Syria, and ultimately stormed Jerusalem. It was the world's "Great Debate": The Crusade.

It was in the last year of the century, July 15, 1099, that the Crusaders had mastered Jerusalem and the Holy Sepulchre and had established their Christian Latin Kingdom almost cutting the Mahommedan world in two. All these outbursts, the new vigor, the reform of the Church, the Norman adventures, the Crusades, inaugurate the strength of the Middle Ages and fill the 11th century with their strength and storm.

The 11th century, the second stage of this rapid advance into the fullness of the high medieval culture, is the century of the main developments. Institutions of which the seeds had been sown generations before, and which had begun to pierce ground in the 11th century, during the 12th become vigorous plants, many of which have endured to this day.

It is the century of the Parliaments, that is, of assemblies representing every class of the community and gathering under the head of the community, the King, in order to arrange what voluntary aid could be given to him for public purposes under some special strain, usually of war. For it must be remembered that there were no taxes as yet in the medieval state. The king was supposed to administer out of the income with which the Crown was endowed, that is, out of his own income, out of the dues he got from his private possessions and from the public land. When something more was exceptionally needed, he had to ask for it from his subjects as a favor and a grant. He could not impose it. Hence Parliaments.

The first of these bodies arose in the little Christian states of the Pyrenees, at that time the most vital provinces of Christendom, because they had borne the brunt of the battle against the Mahommedan. The earliest known and recorded Parliament of Europe is to be found right back in the 11th century: the Parliament of Huesca, long before the Norman Conquest of England. From the Pyrenees the institution spread northward and even appears fully formed at last in England, usually the latest province of the West to receive any new institution. There was no full Parliament in England until the latter part of the 13th century.

Another influence spreading with the 12th century was vernacular literature. There had always been poems and pious writings in the tongue of the populace, side by side with the main Latin language of the West in which all important records and dates were set down. These popular dialects, which we call today "vernacular," were especially lively in Britain, where there was a whole Anglo-Saxon literature that did not die out till a lifetime after the Norman Conquest. In the most of Christendom, the vernacular literature begins to bulk in this 12th century, having already appeared two lifetimes before in epic songs. The 12th century also saw a revolution in architecture. It produced the pointed arch, the ogive, a feature characteristic of all Western Christendom henceforward. This arose in the district of Paris, spread thence throughout France and England, from the Valley of the Rhine to northern Spain, supplanting the old round arch (Romanesque) of the Dark Ages.

It is with the 12th century that you get a new enthusiasm for the higher learning and its debates. The great schools begin to gather in Italy and in Gaul, and in Spain and in the Rhine valleys and in Europe. They become the universities of which Paris was perhaps the most famous. It is the leaders of thought therein and the great debates between them, such as the conflict between Abelard and St. Bernard, which gave life to the foundation of this new thing. Then again the 12th century shows the first beginnings, very vague and tentative, not yet fully conscious, of *national* units in Christendom following the ruling houses. It is the moment of the Plantagenets, the men who were not only independent kings of England, but virtually independent rulers of half France, rivals to the French kings who were in feudal theory their overlords. No man in Europe as yet thought of himself in terms of nationality. A man thought of himself in terms of holding from this or that lord, ultimately from this or that great overlord. But that local spirit which was later on to make the nations of Europe, had already begun to arise in the greater part of united Christendom.

But perhaps the most striking thing about the 12th century was the continued growth of the Papal power. It had challenged those lay encroachments which had marked the Dark Ages. It had, as we have seen, challenged the German tutelage of the Roman See, and now in the next lifetime, it was affirming with all its strength the doctrine of Church investiture.

In no field was the struggle more violent. The old right of the Church to govern itself, to consecrate its own officers, to form a completely free, self-governing corporation coincident with Christendom was offended by the claim to clerical power of local kings, and especially of the chief civil power, the Emperor, ultimate ruler over Italy and the Germanies. The Papacy maintained that, though great bishops and abbots were feudal lords, the Church and the Church alone could decide upon their office. Only the Pope could *invest* the candidate bishop with his office. But, all society having become feudal, great bishoprics and abbacies were lords over masses of lay land, and, what is more, were liable for armed forces when the king issued a summons for such. Therefore, it seemed essential that the king should invest the bishops also. In the end there was a compromise. The spiritual power invested the candidates with the spiritual revenues of their sees or abbeys; the lay power invested them with their lay revenue. In practice, the appointment as well as the investiture of these powerful officials lay with the lay government, but they were not and could not be appointed without the consent of the Papacy as well. And here as in everything else, the tie was made for the strengthening of the See of Rome.

With the institutions in the Middle Ages thus rapidly growing, the whole of its life becoming more and more secure, more confident of its own strength and order, we reach after the year 1200—that is in the 13th century—the flowering time of our race.

The 13th century was that moment in which the high Middle Ages reached their summit. It was that moment in which the Catholic culture came, in the civic sense of the word "culture," to maturity. It was probably the supreme moment of our blood, at any rate one of the very greatest moments. Never had we had such a well-founded society before, never have we since had any society so well founded or so much concerned with justice. A proof, if proof were needed, of the greatness of that time is the scale of the chief public characters, which passed before us already named: St. Louis the King, St. Ferdinand of Castile, St. Dominic and St. Francis, with their new orders of friars; Edward I of England; and, in philosophy, which determines all, the towering name of St. Thomas Aquinas. He established during that great time a body of coördinated doctrine and philosophy which no one had yet possessed. The scale of his work is on a par with its cultural value, and he seemed to have put his seal upon the civilization which he adorned, and, through his establishment of right reason in philosophy, his marriage of Catholicism with the Aristotelian wisdom, to set up a structure that would endure forever and give a norm to our civilization.

It was not destined to establish us in so much peace. We were fated to continue the perpetual changes of Europe. The 13th century, which felt itself to be (as it was) the prime moment of our blood, suffered from our common mortality, and, in the first years of the 14th century a decline had begun. Yet we had some right to boast of a spiritual and political security which was established apparently forever, and of a Christian civilization which will endure indefinitely. The last great effort to destroy Christian society from within, the Albigensian movement, had been crushed and that power which was the main external enemy to the spirit of the Church in Europe, the genius of Frederick II the Emperor, "The Marvel of the World" *(Stupor Mundi)* was also defeated.

That century did, indeed, commit at its outset one

grievous blunder, the consequences of which we still feel
in the apparent impossibility of reconciling the Greek
Church with the Latin and of achieving the unity of both
under the Papacy. This heavy blunder was the expedition
wrongly called the Fourth Crusade. It set out nominally
in aid of Constantinople and for the recovery of the Holy
Land, which had been lost to the Turks. From such a
purpose, the true tradition of all the Crusades, it was
deflected by the government of Venice, without which the
Crusade could have had no transports. Constantinople
owed money to the Venetian Republic, which was the
banking state of the day. To recover that debt, Venice
used the crusading army, bringing it up the Bosphorus
against the Imperial City. The Western or Latin Christians won, they forced the Latin liturgy upon the shrines
of the Greek capital, saying the Latin Mass on the altar
of St. Sophia itself, so supplanting the Greek rite. But
they had wounded the Greek-speaking and Greek-worship-
ing world of the Christian East as deeply as a wound could
pierce. There is a traditional sentence in which that violently and justly roused animosity expressed itself: "Better
a devil on the altar of St. Sophia than a Roman Cardinal
pontificating there."

The so-called Fourth Crusade only imposed the Latin
Mass and a Latin government precariously. The experiment did not last a lifetime. All had reverted to Greek
usage and liturgy well before the end of the century; but
the injustice had been committed, hatred had been planted
in a fiercer form than ever before between Constantinople
and Europe, and the hopes of unity were destroyed, apparently forever. There was, indeed, official effort at
unity in the very last mortal crisis when the Imperial City
on the Bosphorus was on the point of falling forever to the
Turk. That formal reconciliation between the Eastern and
the Western churches is pompously recorded in the very

stones of Florence as though it were immutable. But all that was really recorded was the epitaph of united Christendom.

In spite of that one great blunder, however, the 13th century *was* what I have called it, a promise of permanent Christian order through justice. It founded a conception of the State which seemed unshakable. All society arranged by status, every man in his place and knowing his place, wealth rendered less odious and even noble by stability and long succession, the well divided property of the now almost free peasantry and the fully free craftsman of the towns guaranteed by guild and village custom, a hierarchy of functions strictly bound in one feudal scheme satisfactory to the political conscience of man, and all that ordered social body guaranteed by the vigorous faith whose officials, the clergy, came from every source in society, enjoyed a moral authority they were not later to know, and performed their mighty function adequately and in full order.

Great monuments of the time remain with us, testifying to its strength and solidity, but still more to that active sense of beauty which is one aspect of the divine. The 13th century was the type of our society to which men in their later distresses turned, to which after all our modern wrongheadedness, disasters are compelling us to turn again today. It is, of course, a folly to see perfection in any human phase. The 13th century suffered from the Fall of Man as does the 20th, and as will every other generation; but it came nearer to the rule of justice on earth than anything effected before or since. It was doomed in the time that was coming, for, though its philosophy was immortal, its instruments being human were riddled with mortality. Even that shining spirit grew old and began to fall. With that failure we shall next deal.

(c) THE DECLINE OF THE MIDDLE AGES

This summit of the medieval culture, the time when Europe was most herself, and when our race was probably at its happiest, was doomed to decline. The most glorious of those three centuries, the 13th, was also the last. Shortly after the year 1300 the change begins. It was a tragic change in spite of the world in which it took place, for it was the loss of that which had been our joy and nearest our perfection. The decline lasts through two centuries, from the beginning of the 14th to the beginning of the 16th, and ends in the shipwreck of the Reformation.

As in the rise of Christendom there was a spiritual process going on side by side with the material one, so also in the decline of Christendom after the year 1300. But the two things were exactly contrasted; in the rise of Christendom, as we have seen, there was a decline of material power; the material side of civilization grew coarser and less efficient; Europe slipped down into the Dark Ages in the generations preceding the end of the 5th century; but meanwhile there was spiritual advance, the founding and consolidating of the Christian world, the conversion of the old Roman Empire and the appearance for the first time in the story of our people of a united, an enthusiastically accepted religion.

In the second contrasted period, the end of the Middle Ages, you have a material advance, an increasing knowledge of the world both by discovery and through the sciences (especially towards the end) ; you have an increase in the arts, painting especially takes on a new form altogether and enters a glory of its own which increases for generations; architecture grows more refined, though at last more fantastic; sculpture especially becomes more glorious and never did it reach a higher level than just when the Middle Ages were dying. But with all this went a spiritual decline which at last worked like a mortal disease in the heart of Christendom and led us to the chaos of the Reformation.

From that blow Christendom never fully recovered. Something was saved, as we know; the Catholic Church, threatened with extinction, survived and maintained a great part of its jurisdiction over most of what had been united Christendom, but a full, unquestioned, general religious culture Europe was not to know again.

The sequence which this spiritual decline followed is marked by various characters, of which five are the most important.

(1) Unity, the very principle of life for Christendom —unity of doctrine and unity of discipline and organization in the field of religion—was shaken.

(2) The organic structure of the Catholic Church was weakened as a consequence, and at the same time begins, as it were, to "ossify," to grow old and dead.

(3) The old living restraints which preserved the body of Christendom from decay and dissolution become more and more mechanical; authority finds itself depending more and more upon force and less and less upon agreement.

(4) Doubts and extravangances, two bad symptoms in any religious scheme, grow in the body of Christendom: doubts not only on doctrine, but also on the titles to authority; extravagances in legends and usages.

(5) The period is marked (especially towards the end) by two complementary evils, necessarily following upon the over-reliance of authority upon force. It is marked by the evil of unworthy officers to preside over and conduct the religion of Christendom, and it is marked by the increasing efforts of those officers to prevent the catastrophe produced by their own insufficiency; so that at last

in the 15th century and early 16th you get something like a religious reign of terror which is bound to exhaust itself and to break down.

All this sounds evil enough, and evil indeed it was, but we must not exaggerate. The deterioration and worsening of religion as the Middle Ages closed, has, since the Reformation, been grossly exaggerated by the permanent enemies of the Catholic Church, and even more by those who without a deliberate motive of hostility, are affected by ignorance and by separation from Catholic tradition.

There was plenty of holy living; there was the full practice of the Faith even in the worst moments at the end of the decline; there was a large body of vital tradition which came at last to save our society after the great quarrel at the close of the Middle Ages had all but destroyed it. Moreover, while this spiritual decline was going on, Europe was filled with an increasing vitality. Men were not only perpetually learning new things and glorying in discovery, but were filled, especially towards the end of the period, with a zest for adventure. There was something creative about the air in which the Middle Ages came to an end; but the forces at work produced nothing permanent.

Christendom was shaken and almost dissolved, but so far from a new inheritance taking its place, divisions among men increased, until we reach the perilous extreme in which we stand today, when our civilization is possessed of greater powers over nature than ever it had before, and yet seems bent on its own destruction.

These five main processes of spiritual decline must be examined in a little more detail if we are to understand them.

I say that in the first place unity was shaken, and that was the underlying grievous thing from which all other evils proceeded. Paradoxically unity was the more shaken because it had been the more thoroughly taken for granted throughout the world; nor was it until disunion had done its full work that men woke up tardily to the vital necessity of unity.

The center and sustenance of Christian unity was the authority of the Apostolic See, and the threat to unity appears precisely there.

In the high Middle Ages there had been a struggle, as we have seen, between the Papacy and the lay power, culminating in the life-and-death conflict between Frederick II and the Pope, who gradually got the better of his scepticism and usurpation.

From this conflict the Papacy emerged victorious. The danger of the Pope's becoming a mere servant of the lay power and of the Emperor, with Germany and Italy behind him, overshadowing and rendering subservient the Christian body of the Latin West (as the Eastern Emperor had overshadowed and rendered subservient the Greek East), was over. But there did not follow, as there promised to follow, a long period of equal balance between the central spiritual Papal power and the lesser powers of the Western Princes—the Kings of England, France, and the rising monarchs of Spain. What followed was the capture of the Papal See by the power of the French monarchy. It had been rescued from becoming a German thing; it became a French thing.

The Popes left Rome, they settled in the town of Avignon which, though not feudally subject to the French King at Paris, was fully in the French culture. For seventy years, that is, the full lifetime of a man, Rome was deserted. A new Papal court, developing a spirit of intricate finance, appeared upon the Rhone, and one after another the Popes at Avignon were chosen from among the French Prelates.

That state of affairs, the central spiritual authority of Christendom captured by one province of Christendom, could not endure. Nor did it. Rival Popes were set up and the Princes of Europe divided their allegiance between one claimant and another as opponents. When two national forces were at war, one would follow the Pope at Avignon and the other would deny that Pope's authority and accept the authority of an anti-Pope. The scandal was not only enormous, but profound. It went to the roots of Christendom; for it must be remembered that all the while the Papal office was regarded as supreme, as being the very heart of Christian society, although men were fighting as to who might properly claim it and although it seemed to have lost the principle of identity. This turmoil has been called "The Great Schism of the West." When at last it was healed and one Pope, accepted by all Christendom, mounted that throne under the title of Martin V, the Papacy was reëstablished indeed in unity, but had most heavily lost in prestige. The Popes were back in Rome, but in peril of becoming mere Italian Princes. All this was the first shaking of unity; the second was the growth of national consciousness.

This new element was not for generations to reach a level in which the ultimate unity of Christendom was forgotten, but it continued to rise, and with every step in the rise of national feeling from obscure half conscious origins to the fierce rivalries at the end of the Middle Ages, the unity of Christendom weakened. The Churches themselves took on a national color; the local hierarchies were not only the creatures of the Princes, but became bodies separate, not of course in doctrine and discipline, but in social habit, as indeed they have since remained, even where unity has been preserved.

I have said that in the second place the organic structure of religion weakened through a sort of ossification. By a metaphor taken from the decline of the human body one might compare the process to the hardening of the arteries: that arterio-sclerosis which is the characteristic mark of age in a living body. You see this in three of its two main effects; in the growth of superstitions, in the warping of history through legends, and, much more serious, in the attitude taken towards the revenues and endowments of religion.

Superstition did not intrench on doctrine. Many write as though it had done so; but those who thus write, write bad history. Doctrine remained clear and distinct and well founded throughout; but the spirit of superstition overlay it. For instance, the doctrine of the Invocation of Saints is clear; but towards the end of the Middle Ages you get men robbing one shrine in order to enrich another. The doctrine of the use of Masses is clear; and especially their use for the benefit of the souls in Purgatory; but the superstition that a Mass in this place was efficacious, and in that, was not—the superstition which confused mechanical repetition with spiritual force, grew as the Middle Ages declined.

The strongest example of the thing is also the best known, because it was the immediate occasion of the final catastrophe; I mean the attitude towards Indulgences.

The defined doctrine is perfectly clear. The authorities of the Church can ascribe the spiritual advantages earned by holy men and women as a sort of fund or surplus for the benefit of others; thus is an indulgence granted. Towards the end of the Middle Ages in popular practice the definition grew dead, and indulgences, with too many people, turned into something like a mechanical service. Where they could be granted by the giving of alms or money for a pious purpose, such as Church-building, too many men thought of them as spiritual benefits that could be bought as medicines can be bought.

Side by side with this went the parallel evil of false history. A legend is essentially a parable, a story told not as a true historical thing, but as a symbol. Legends were of the utmost value through the beauty with which they were clothed, and even of value through their humor; but they did harm instead of good when they began to be taken as historical realities. And men were often more attached to a local legend which gave them a false idea of their own past than to the general truths of religion. Neither a measure of superstition nor a measure of legend mistaken for truth is mortal, but an excess of either can be mortal; because men reacting against such excesses will react against the whole body of religion. We know how, after the great quarrel against the Church as a whole had broken out, a vast mass of true history came to be treated as legendary, and a vast mass of essential doctrine and practice came to be treated as superstitious through reaction against extravagances of an earlier time.

But, as I have said, the worst symptom of all was the way in which Church endowment came to be treated as the Middle Ages drew to a close. The religion of Christendom which had slowly made our civilization until it had culminated in the brilliant climax of the High Middle Ages, had been from the beginning endowed. Even when the Catholic Church was no more than an unpopular, though vigorous, half-concealed society within the old Pagan Empire it had had a regular organization of funds which, though the civil authorities did not then approve of the Church, were protected by law. It has always been an instinct of the Church to guard its life by economic independence.

When Catholicism became the accepted and universal religion, endowments were largely increased and established. There was a revenue for each diocese, of course, supporting the Bishop and his activities, and a revenue for the parishes as they were formed; and these endowments were fixed in shape of rents from land. There were also dues payable, tithes of produce from the fields. The monasteries were endowed with land by pious foundation or the contributions of their original members.

As the Christian centuries proceeded this accumulation of landed wealth in the hands of the Church got greater and greater; hospitals were endowed under Church patronage, so were all places of education—the local schools, and later the universities and their colleges. To every clerical function, direct or indirect—to a prebend, a canonry, a village presbytery, a monastery, a foundation for Masses, a hospital, etc.—there was its own fixed revenue coming in from the dues paid upon land by those who held it of the lord of the land. The lord was in this case the clerical unit concerned, the See or prebend or college or monastery or what not. By the end of the Middle Ages through this perpetual accumulation (from which there was very little leakage) the totals had grown enormous. It is commonly said that one-third of the wealth of Europe was thus clerical.

The phrase is ambiguous, for the total wealth of a country includes the livelihood of everybody in it; what was really meant was that one-third of the surplus values or rents and dues went to Church endowment of one kind and another, including education, hospitals, certain resthouses on the great roads of travel, etc., and only the remaining two-thirds went as revenues to lay lords of all kinds. Possibly that popular estimate is exaggerated; possibly even at the very end of the Middle Ages (say in the year 1500), the total surplus values in clerical hands was not more than a quarter of the whole. But even that was a formidable proportion to be set aside for the support of men who were but a small minority in the State, though a minority who during all their useful period were carrying out vast and essential public functions.

Now the characteristic corruption at the end of the Middle Ages was that these endowments *came to be treated as mere sources of private income.* They had been intended as means for the support of that active, useful and necessary soul of society, the Church. But the means came to be taken for the end, and they were more and more treated as we treat stocks and shares and bonds today. Men invested in them; a man would buy a prebend for a child of his, and virtually buy an abbacy or the superiorship of a nunnery, which carried with it a large endowment, for his daughter. A Bishopric would be given by a king to a favorite by way of providing him with an income. Again, the man enjoying the revenues of, say, a Bishopric, would not be content with that, but would hold at the same time another Bishopric, or even perhaps two or three, keeping the revenues for himself and paying a much lesser sum to a subordinate: "farming out" the Church revenues in this fashion. Worse still, it became quite common for some great abbey to be given to a layman *in commendam.* This thoroughly irreligious system became in some countries (such as Scotland) almost universal. What had been in the past a great Benedictine Abbey with, say, a hundred thousand dollars a year of revenue, would be handed over to the bastard of a king or any other kind of favorite who would put in a paid agent to act as abbot, while he himself kept the bulk of the revenue under the legal fiction that he was the "guardian" of the establishment. In general, all over Christendom men saw these vast sums which had been set aside for the proper conduct of the Church, for alms to the poor, for education, medicine, etc., used as private fortunes, and often so used not even by clerics, but by laymen.

Here again we must not exaggerate; the evil was very great and it was everywhere, but it was not universal. The great bulk of the Church's income still continued to be used for the right purposes; for the conduct of the liturgy, the upkeep of the churches, colleges, hospitals, schools, etc. But towards the end of the Middle Ages men had grown used to the scandal of religious or quasi-religious endowment being thought of as so much private revenue to be used indifferently for the right purposes or the wrong. It may be imagined how increasingly the mass of men (who are poor and to whom the Church should act as succor, guardian and guide) resented the abuse. It was one of the chief sources of the explosion that was to follow.

Another step to be noticed in the process of disintegration going on within Christendom, was the growth of doubt: disturbance and uncertainty on what had once been certainly held doctrines, believed in by all Society. New physical discovery had a lot to do with the spread of this spirit; even geographical discovery, which began to expand as the Middle Ages declined, helped to disturb men's minds on the nature of the universe; and corruption among the clergy disturbed men's minds on the validity of the Sacraments. It began to be maintained that a Sacrament was not valid unless the officer of the Church administering it was in the state of grace, and it was but a step from this to saying that the sacramental power of the clergy was an illusion. That was at the back of the movement with which in England the name of Wycliffe was connected.

Especially did doubts upon the Real Presence grow, until they spread to great masses of the populace. A sort of universal tendency to heresy was "in the air" as the Middle Ages proceeded to their close; and side by side with it there went what seems to be the universal accompaniments of doubt, superstition and extravagant practices. We have mentioned the abuse of indulgences. The visiting and cultus of relics also coupled with payments, perilously approached in the popular mind the conception of mere purchase: the buying and selling of spiritual power. The vast extension of Masses said for the dead, got entangled with these extravagant ideas. Meanwhile the growth of scholarship and the critical spirit, exploding legends and false doctrines on every side, continued to weaken the structure of religion.

An excellent example of this was the "Donation of Constantine." There is no doubt that Constantine in moving the capital of the Empire to Byzantium left in the West great political powers to the Bishop of Rome; but a document which purported to confirm special powers under the hand of the Emperor and known as the "Donation" was quoted as genuine, though marked by fantastic fables. It was not the foundation of the Papal temporal power, but it had been used in confirmation of it, so that when it was proved to be legendary the respect for the Papacy was shaken.

The last feature of the decline was that which has stood out vividly in the mind of posterity more than any other and to this day the enemies of the Catholic Church emphasize it more violently than anything else. It was this: As moral authority weakened, mechanical restraint strengthened.

It is always so; the use of force, punishment, threat and fear are necessary for the keeping of order and the maintenance of right laws in action. But in a healthy state of affairs much the greater part of the strength of authority is moral. Men obey because they think they ought to obey; because they feel that the authority which governs them has a right to do so. As moral authority weakens those who exercise authority tend to fall back upon physical restraint, punishment, and the mere fear of consequences as a method of administration. That is what happened towards the end of the Middle Ages in the matter of heresy in every form, and not only of heresy but of rebellions or even grumblings against the powers of the clergy. We have said with little exaggeration that the end of the Middle Ages was a "religious reign of terror." In the older and simpler days capital punishment seemed a natural consequence of heresy because heresy was an attempt to break up that Christian society by which all men lived. It was at once a treason and a murder, and the people themselves were quite ready to exercise it if the regular authorities were slack, just as today men will take the law into their own hands by lynching if they think that justice will not be done in a matter where they feel strongly. But later on, in the efforts to maintain spiritual authority, everywhere attacked and losing its moral sanctions, the officers of the Church fell back upon increasing severity and frequency of restraint by fear.

The burning of people alive as a punishment was a thing of very old establishment; dating back for more than a thousand years right into the Roman Empire.* It was a civil punishment only occasionally used, but none the less familiar to men's minds. It was attached to certain heinous crimes quite apart from religion, for instance, coining— that is, the making of false money. But towards the end of the Middle Ages its use became extravagant and the spirit of it continued long after the Reformation, as for instance its use against witchcraft, and against those who in Spain were conspiring against the State. This evil, the association of violence and horrible punishment with the maintenance of orthodoxy, grew rapidly throughout the end of the decline; and nothing did more to provoke that violent outburst to follow, in which the unity of Christendom was broken assunder.

* For instance: Julian the Apostate burnt alive officials who had refused to betray his rival.

Let us end by considering in the critical spirit applied to document and tradition, the probable causes of that general spiritual decline, accompanied as it was by steady advance in knowledge and mastery over the material world.

It is always very difficult to ferret out the causes of any great social movement; because its roots lie deep and hidden, stretching far into the past; and with all that, are invariably complicated and entangled. But it may fairly be said that the main cause of the decline was old age; mortality. Any human institution being administered by mortals is in peril continually of that fate.

The Church itself was regarded and will continue to be regarded by its adherents as immortal, but its administration is subject to perpetual threat of mortality, that is of corruption and weakness tending to extinction; in vigorous periods the tendency is as strong as in periods of weakness; only, in vigorous periods, it is countered by perpetual watchfulness and readiness to reform, whereas when the soul of Society is sick the counteraction weakens. In the high Middle Ages the tendency to all that would weaken Christendom was vigorously countered; in the later Middle Ages it was allowed to grow and given greater and greater play, combated by mechanical means of repression, rather than by vigorous spiritual self-examination and self-discipline.

Next we find as a cause the disintegrating effect of rapid discovery, especially towards the end of the process. When the spiritual life is vigorous it can deal with, absorb, digest, no matter what novel truth. Thus the coming of a restored Greek philosophy and some measure of Greek learning upon Western Christendom of the 12th century was a disturbance due to discovery, to the expansion of what may be called in the largest sense of the word "science." It proffered an example of what we find successively throughout every period of human expansion, the conflict between religion and science; that is between spiritual concepts and the clothing thereof in particular forms which prove untenable under the light of further knowledge. The true Middle Ages dealt strongly with the new knowledge, digested it, incorporated it, and in the high climax of that civilization St. Thomas became the exponent of Aristotle, and married his philosophy to the theology of the Church Universal. But with the later Middle Ages the power to do all this declined.

As the voyages of discovery, begun with the 14th century, expanded men's knowledge of the world in which they lived, that expansion of knowledge disturbed their fixed habits of thought upon the universe. So did each new invention as applied to travel and to the arts. There is no logical connection between the expansion of temporal knowledge and the loss of spiritual certitude; but the expansion of knowedge interferes with fixed habits of mind, and among these are the forms which spiritual certitude takes. The discovery that what was thought historical truth is in reality a legend; that what had been thought a genuine relic was false; that what had been thought a genuine document was a romance or a forgery, did not invalidate the doctrine of relics, nor true documents, nor sound tradition; but by an association of ideas the advance of such discovery shook the ordinary mind in its grasp of truth.

Among the new instruments thus at work which proved of most violent effect was that of printing. The press created a sort of new false authority. It would present speculation in the form of affirmed fact and, what is more important, it would *proclaim that fact to many minds at the same moment and in the same form.* Printing diffused true knowledge, but it also diffused (and perhaps on a greater scale) false knowledge and unproved irrational affirmation. Among other things it gave vastly added strength to the irrational concept that a document is alone important to the proof of anything in the past, and that tradition may be neglected. From that error we still suffer every day; men forget that tradition, though it gets warped with time and tends to be diverse and vague is commonly sincere; whereas a document may be, and if official, commonly is, deliberately false.

Another obvious cause of social and therefore spiritual decline in the end of the Middle Ages was the dragging out of the interminable raids called "The Hundred Years' War." The French-speaking Kings of England had a much better claim to the inheritance of the crown of France in the 14th century than the textbooks usually allow. They pursued that claim with the idea of founding a great Western monarchy to include both France and England. The effort failed, but not until it had dragged on for a hundred years bringing poverty and misery, wherever the armies marched, from the first main conflict at Crecy just before the middle of the 14th century, to the expulsion of the English garrisons in Normandy more than a hundred years later.

But what had more effect than these and twenty other possible causes that might be invoked, was the pestilence now known (it was not so called at the time) as the Black Death.

Pestilence was recurrent; but the Black Death was, as it were, the extra drop that made the cup run over. It was a visitation upon a scale so enormous as to strike a blow at medieval society which might have dissolved it—and nearly did dissolve it. Certainly a third of Western Christendom died within two years in the middle of the 14th century; in many places there is sufficient proof that half the population disappeared. In some places towns and villages sank never to rise again. It was a form of bubonic plague which had spread from the east and ran through the ports of the Mediterranean, so northward through France to England, even to the extremes of European colonization in Greenland; and everywhere you may trace its effects even today in the half finished buildings which were stopped dead and completion never undertaken. Beauvais is one example of this, so is the Cathedral of Narbonne, so is the parish Church of Great Yarmouth in England, and there are hundreds of similar examples scattered up and down the face of Western Europe.

The various divisions of Christendom were still further separated by this violent calamity. Through it the English language came into existence. The children of the French-speaking wealthier classes in England could no longer be trained on account of lack of teachers in the tradition of French speech. There came about therefore, a fusion between what had been the language of the governing classes of centuries and the various mixed dialects (mainly Germanic) of the populace; of the servants, that is, by whom the richer children were brought up and of the village lad with whom they played. The Black Death not only thus cut off England from Europe, but also relaxed travel everywhere and alienated district from district. It struck Europe with a wound which might have been mortal, and from which, as a fact, its unity and moral health never fully recovered.

All these things combined accompanied or led to the breakdown of that high spiritual civilization whose crown had been the 13th century. Beauty was better served on every side, architecture though it became somewhat fantastic and less strong was certainly more detailed and lovely; painting became an exquisite art; the vernacular literatures began to take on a new glory of their own, and it is significant that the greatest monument of these, the mighty poem of Dante, was coincident with the spiritual misfortunes of the decline.

Such was the process, and such apparently the causes of the process. As the result of that process there accumulated an element of instability; a strain which clamored for solution and a tension which became unbearable. Everything was ready for an explosion: and the explosion took place.

III

THE REFORMATION AND ITS IMMEDIATE CONSEQUENCES

We have seen how the Middle Ages declined on their spiritual side and how the clerical organization, that is, the temporal structure of the Church, was becoming ossified and ceasing to function properly; was raising opposition of every kind; was provoking the anger of those who felt they were not being spiritually fed, the anger of those who contrasted the spiritual functions for which endowment had been made with the characters of those who received the incomes of those endowments. We have noted the spiritual starvation of great numbers of the laity; the absence of predication, and so forth.

We have seen how it was inevitable that under such conditions specific heresies should arise, and that, since the growing quarrel was specially a quarrel with the clerical organization of the Church (that is, with the monasteries, with the parish endowments and those of the cathedral Sees and Bishoprics, with pluralities, or the holding of many endowments by one person, and so forth), the main heresies arose upon the point of hierarchical authority and the special claims and position of the whole Church organization. It was essentially a rising *anti-clerical* tide, and therefore the heresies took the form of attacking the powers and claims of the priesthood and of the Papacy, which was the summit and coping stone of the whole clerical body.

Thus there were heresies beginning in the 14th century, as we have seen, protesting that the Sacraments could not be validly administered nor even the Host consecrated save by priests in the state of grace. There were heresies denying the right of the Church and its various organizations—the monasteries, etc.—to hold property at all. There were heresies especially attacking, at first somewhat timidly, the doctrine of the Real Presence, because it was the power of the priest to consecrate which was at the basis of his special sacred position—and against this was protest arising. In general, there was this spirit of anti-unity abroad, and it was exasperated by the dilatory policy of the authorities in the Church. There was perpetual cry for a reform, a thorough cleansing of the whole society, a return to the great virtues which had marked the earlier Middle Ages. But nothing sufficient was done until it was too late.

It is nearly always so in the great catastrophes of mankind. There is nearly always ample warning. There are many and even violent preliminary shocks like the preliminary shocks of a great earthquake or volcanic eruption. They incommode and even frighten those whose position or privileges are threatened. But they hardly ever sufficiently incommode or frighten them to spur them into necessary action. The truth is that the end of the Middle Ages was, as I said, a sort of religious "Reign of Terror." The growing rebellion was met by legal method, the use of force, continued and often fearful punishments, but, not by that spiritual change which the times demanded.

A special instance of what was going on will illustrate all this better than generalities:

One of the chief grievances which raised men's anger against the organization of the Church was the payment of *mortuaries*—that is, dues payable upon death. When a man died, say a substantial farmer in any district, such and such a part of the clerical organization had the right of burying him and of collecting the dues which followed upon his death. For instance, the parish would ordinarily have the right to bury him, and whoever owned the parish dues (which in the course of time had become immensely complicated—various forms of tithes, etc., fees payable on particular occasions and all the rest of it) would collect funeral dues from the family after the funeral. But apart from that there were payments in kind at a death which varied with different places and with local customs. In some places the mortuary took the form of appropriating the most valuable individual object discoverable in the dead man's house, a jewel, for instance, or a good piece of furniture. In practice, of course, the thing was compounded for, since payment was made to redeem it, but the whole system was irritating and the exasperation was all the greater because it no longer corresponded to anything real in the organization of Society. It appeared no more than a senseless tax for swelling the revenues of the clergy at the expense of the laity. These mortuaries might have been compounded, bought up by public arrangement and gradually extinguished, but those who benefited by them were too numerous and the customs attached to them too diverse for any common action to be taken. The governments of the various parts of Christendom had only local powers over temporal affairs; the Church affairs and the Church reforms were something quite separate. Civil government could not touch them and the complaints, however violent, could find no appreciable redress from the king and his laws. In connection with this we can understand the bitter feeling that had arisen about the power of the ecclesiastical courts.

The ecclesiastical courts had arisen under the simple conditions of the early Middle Ages for the trial of cases purely spiritual. They were presided over by the Bishop or his deputies, not by the civil officers of the community. They inquired into heresies, they dealt with matrimonial cases, with wills, with dues payable to ecclesiastical bodies. Their decisions were naturally in favor of increasing as much as possible the revenues drawn by the clerical side of Society from laymen; they had become in the corruption of the later Middle Ages engines too often used for extortion. It was always an advantage to the ecclesiastical lawyers and ecclesiastical judges to discover cases of heresy or spiritual misdemeanor in order to increase revenue by fines and the rest, as also to increase the power of their organization.

A famous case was that of Hunn, an important London citizen, who tacked on to the vernacular translation of the Scriptures a preface denouncing, among other things, forms of revenue whereby the Papacy benefited, especially indulgences. He was arrested and held in the prisons of the Bishop of London, and there his body was found dead. He probably died a natural death, but seeing how tempers were exasperated at the time there was rumor, of course, of suicide and even of murder. That is only one instance, and an extreme one, but it will serve to explain the increasing ill ease under which Christendom lived.

At the same time, men began to lose their respect for their ecclesiastical superiors. I have given instances of how the Church at the end of the Middle Ages would foster such a feeling. The Church had originated as an instrument of divine persuasion, it had flourished by its power of conversion and edification. When its human instruments began to give so much repeated scandal it was in peril of subversion.

In other words, a pile of gunpowder had been accumulating, at any moment a match might be set to the train and an explosion would follow in which the unity of Christendom would be destroyed.

The decisive moment might have fallen at almost any time in the last 150 years of the Middle Ages from the days of Wycliffe and then of Huss to the end of the 15th century. As a fact, the moment which accidentally proved the origin of the final breakup was in the later part of the year 1517, when an eloquent man of confused mind but great energy, an Augustinian monk called Martin Luther, proposed to debate in the University of Wittenberg the whole theory of indulgences. The occasion was the offering of indulgences throughout Germany accompanied by a demand for alms. Much of the money so gathered was to be used for the new building of St. Peter's in Rome; much for the recoupment of speculators; but the occasion was accidental.

In the temper of the moment almost anything might have produced catastrophe. All Germany was filled with a violent tumult. In Spain and France where the indulgence had not been preached or travelled, the emotions were less strong, but among the Germans there was a fever of excitment. It was partly due, of course, to the new national and racial feelings which had been growing as the unity of the Middle Ages decayed. It was partly an emphasis on the contrast between the German and the Italian. It was in the main an anarchic, diverse, loud, confused protest, not possessed of any positive principle save an attack upon the general principle of unity and upon the hierarchical organization of the Church: particularly, therefore, an attack upon the claims to authority of the Pope.

As a mere negative heretical movement wherein a mass of divergent and even contradictory opinions had free play, the movement might have been less destructive. But there was a driving power behind it which was of very great effect; the opportunity for loot. Here were these great monastic establishments, the numbers enjoying which had dwindled, but the revenues of which had been maintained. The Papacy was the central authority. Deny the authority of the Papacy and it lay defenseless before attack and spoliation. Such attack followed almost immediately upon the first years of the great revolt. Certain of the Swiss cantons and the more or less independent small secular princes especially in the north of Germany, certain of the Free Cities, as they were called (that is, the mercantile corporations of the trading towns), these and even local squires and petty lordlings fell upon the endowments of religious houses and of parishes, of Sees and all forms of clerical income, swelling their own fortunes out of the proceeds. It may be imagined what a temptation lay before all those not restrained by a governmental power above them to indulge this orgy of loot.

Nevertheless, it may fairly be said that the explosion would not have had a constructive result but for the appearance about ten years after the first Lutheran protest of a book—and behind that book a mind—which was to dominate all the future of the rebellion against Catholic unity.

It was a book from the pen of a certain northern Frenchman, by name Jean Cauvin, or Chauvin, in the Latin Calvinus, whom his followers now know everywhere as John Calvin. He it was who erected a counter-church well organized and defined and therefore capable of expansion and endurance. He set up as the foundation of that church a surely developed, well expounded and argued philosophical system which is still so well known as to need no special description here. It is enough to say that he recognized only one will in the universe—the Divine Will—that he tended, therefore, to ascribe not only good, but evil operations to that Will and emphasized the Divine Majesty so strongly as to get the right relations of God to man out of proportion; that he weakened in man—one may say virtually denied—the power of free will, stressing out of reason (but with powerful effect) the role of predestination. Man's good deeds proceeding from no free will were of no effect towards the salvation of man's soul. Inspired by this general doctrine was to be organized a new Church which was actually the creation of Calvin's mind, but which he and his followers enthusiastically built up, on the plea that it was a return to what the true Church had been in its original purity. He proposed an ecclesiastical system in which each congregation elected its minister, the corporation of ministers forming a synod or collective body summonable upon occasion and the whole body of clergy and laity so defined constituting what he called "the Church," the whole thing being built up of individual congregations which were called "the Churches."

Within these the Eucharist continued in a form, the exact definition of which was still debated, but which excluded the old sacramental idea as idolatrous—in other words, Calvin's construction destroyed and abhorred the Mass, which had been from immemorial time everywhere the central act of Christendom.

Like all the other reformers, he set up, but with more precision than many of them, the Scriptures as the sole rule of faith, accepting by a curious irony, for an absolute authority that which could in the nature of things have no authority at all, save for the tradition of the Catholic Church he was attacking. For no one in all these centuries would have regarded the Scriptures as possessing Divine authority or would have called them the word of God had not the Catholic Church insisted on that mystical doctrine. It was even the Church which had decided what should be and should not be included within the term Scripture.

The strength of Calvin's action, therefore, and his creative power, lay in the strictly logical, orderly, and defined arrangement of his new body. It grew through its local churches and their enthusiastic adherents much as Communism today grows, by cells, and though it was democratic in appeal through its system of election, yet it was excessively authoritative in practice through its superadded doctrine that the officers on which that army depended—that is, the ministers of the Church, the elected presbyters—once elected and ordained, could no longer be questioned. Calvin stands thus at the origin of a whole group of interconnected modern ideas which have had the greatest effect upon the developments of politics and philosophy in the centuries following.

Thus the parliamentary institution which is now increasingly distasteful to the European mind derives ultimately from Calvin, for it is based on the idea of electing a deputy and then giving that deputy absolute power over the electors. Again the Monist conception, the idea that all things are one and that spiritual and material forces have the same root—the philosophy underlying modern materialist science—derives from Calvin's doctrine of there being only one will in the universe. Indirectly (as we shall see later) a consequence of even greater importance followed from Calvin's definitions and the powerful organization he inspired. For it is to these that ultimately the growth of Capitalism can be traced, against which today the whole world is in revolt.

The effect of Calvin herein is indirect, but none the less strong. In denying the efficacy of good deeds and of the human will, of abnegations, in leaving on one side as useless all the doctrine and tradition of Holy Poverty, Calvin opened the door to the domination of the mind by money. St. Thomas had said it centuries before—that if men abandoned the idea of God as the supreme good they would tend to replace Him by the idea, implicit, not directly stated, but of high practical effect, that material wealth is the supreme good. Calvin never said in so many words, and indeed, never thought that men should principally pursue the accumulation of wealth, but he broke down the barriers which Catholicism had erected against that perilous force, and, following on his action, Christendom began to turn to the idea of wealth as at least the only certain good, and therefore the main thing to be aimed at.

Calvin himself would have said with learning, sincerity, and zeal that the glory of God was the only object worthy of human activity, but as he divorced such activity from the power of saving the individual soul, what could there remain save the pursuit of riches?

Calvin began his predication in his native France and there issued his first appeal in the shape of a strong letter to the French King. Attacked at once as heretical, he joined the Swiss reformers and became the master of the independent republic of Geneva, with which town his name will always be specially connected.

It is to be remembered that his first movement against the orthodox Church and its hierarchy began in a family quarrel. His father had been the wealthy lawyer who looked after the affairs of the diocese of Noyon, a very rich royal Bishopric northeast of Paris. He was accused to the Bishop and his chapter of embezzling the funds that passed through his hands and asked to deliver his accounts. He refused and was excommunicated. Young John Calvin himself, the son for whom his father had bought a block of clerical revenue, was despoiled of it on account of the quarrel and was the more angry with the local clerical authorities. But it would be unjust and bad history to make this original dispute, though there was involved in it a money question, which always embitters every quarrel, the main cause of Calvin's rebellion. It was the occasion of that rebellion, but not the motive power.

When we survey the effect of Calvin over the general body of Christendom, we find that France became the battlefield for the triumph or defeat of Calvin's system. Its military quality and its precision appealed to Calvin's fellow-countrymen, and for a lifetime the leaders of the French nation were first of all divided and finally engaged in the most violent civil conflict to decide whether Calvinism should or should not direct the future of the nation. The town of Paris turned the scale; it was intensely devoted to the tradition of Catholicism and compelled the Calvinist leader (who was also the heir to the throne, Henry of Navarre) at the end of the civil wars to accept Catholicism. But the Calvinists under the name of Huguenots remained vigorous and numerous—more than half the higher nobility of France and the great mass of squires, many also of the wealthy middle class, the population of certain seaports, and even groups of peasantry, especially in the mountain districts such as the Cevennes. The ferment of Huguenotry—that is, of Calvinism—worked in the body of the nation. It was to produce later on among the Catholics themselves the movement known as Jansenism, and in the long run it may be found at the root of the skepticism which became so strong at the end of the 17th and grew through the 18th century. It is also at the root of the strong anti-Catholic political and social feeling which was long of such powerful effect upon the French mind and still divides the nation bitterly.

In England Calvinism was of no such effect. Although

in Scotland it swept the field, in England the authorities were reluctant to accept its political and clerical structure. It did produce now, even in England, the large and enthusiastic minority of Puritans who had such power in the earlier 17th century, two lifetimes after Calvin's death, but it never wholly occupied the English mind.

What separated England from Catholic unity was no enthusiasm for the Calvinist system, but the vested interest which the wealthier class in England soon had in supporting the Reformation doctrines; it was because they had received the loot of the monasteries and other clerical endowment, as we shall see later on.

Among the Germans there was division. The main Reformation movement among the Germans was not Calvinist, it was Lutheran, occupied with local independence much more than with fixed and defined doctrine, directed against the central authority of the empire (already badly weakened) much more than towards any new Church or accepted system of doctrine. In general you may say that, after the explosion, the spiritual ruins of what had been Christendom lay in three sets. In one, Catholic tradition had been maintained in spite of the storm. Society pulled itself together, tightened up the bonds of clerical authority, and did all the work we associate with the Council of Trent. The Emperor at Vienna, the French monarchy remained Catholic. Against them was a smaller but advancing Protestant Europe, principally of the north (but counting a powerful faction in France), having for its chief political center the new Protestant government of England. And that Protestant culture thus arising was divided into two groups—the Calvinist with its strict organization maintained what may be called the essence of Protestantism, alive. Side by side with it, less definite, equally anti-Catholic, but for political rather than doctrinal reasons, lay the German Lutherans and the new English organization which retained many ecclesiastical titles of the old Catholic world, but had definitely adopted the Protestant ethic, which was ranged against the remains of Catholic Europe.

What I have called "the explosion," that sudden break-up and change for which the common name is the Reformation (the resolving of the increasing strain under which the last of medieval society had fallen at the very end of the Middle Ages), produced revolutionary results in every department of human life.

The whole of European Christian society was at once shaken and transformed. What had been for centuries a Christian and therefore satisfactory equilibrium in human relations gradually developing a free peasantry in the place of the old slave-state, ordering by rule and custom the economic structure of Society, regarding men as connected by status, rather than by contract, guarding against excessive competition, insistent upon stability, disappeared as a result of the mighty shock delivered in the early 16th century. There came in the place of the old stable medieval civilization which had latterly grown increasingly *unstable,* and in place of the old social philosophy which for centuries had satisfied mankind, a new state of affairs the various parts of which developed at various rates, but all of which combined, came in the long run, to form the modern world. And this is the condition from which we are only now emerging: a social state based upon unbridled competition, one eliminating the old idea of status and regarding only contract, and presenting towards its close that phenomenon of industrial capitalism, the revolt against which now threatens to destroy civilization itself.

Let it be remembered that all the while the material side of civilization was advancing; a wider knowledge of the physical world through the advance of science and geographical discovery, a more critical spirit applied to history and documents, sacred and profane, an intellectual "clearing," as it has been called, went side by side with the breakdown of all by which Christians had hitherto lived.

That paradox must always be borne in mind as we follow those effects of the change which medieval Catholic society (and, for that matter, most men now of our own time) would deplore.

For while we were losing what was spiritually of the highest value, we were gaining on the material side constantly in a continuous advance which has not reached its limit even today. The power of man over nature, his knowledge of the external detail, at least, (though not of the inward nature) of the world to which he belongs, were all on an ascending grade, even as the philosophy on which he had so long reposed was failing him. If we forget these material advantages which grew side by side with the spiritual decline, we shall get our general view out of proportion and fail to understand why many men, perhaps most men, still regard the transformation of Europe, in spite of the perils into which it has at last led us, as an advantage to the race.

Let us consider the effects of that great transformation in two successive aspects—the political and the economic —and take those aspects in that order, dealing with the political first and the economic last.

This is indeed to reverse the order which almost all men of the 19th century and most men today would follow, for in the 19th century it was taken for granted that economic phenomena in society, that is, the way in which wealth is produced, distributed and exchanged, were the causes of political change. And even today most men still cling to that conception.

But the conception is false; political change invariably

comes prior to economic change; economic change could not take place but for the acceptation of laws and a machinery of government which allows the new economic conditions to function. First comes in every great revolution of European affairs, a spiritual change; next, bred by this, a change in social philosophy and therefore in political arrangement; lastly, the economic change which political rearrangement has rendered possible.

There were two political conceptions at war after the unity of Christendom had been shattered by the Reformation: That which clung to the memory of the old common European State called Christendom—that common European Polity had cherished the very unity which was being denied and partially ruined; and now arising a *new* conception of the world, in which each district or realm should enjoy absolute independence and each have the power to make laws applicable to all its citizens, without any interference from a superior moral power.

The old ideal of unity in Christendom had been expressed through two main institutions, the Empire and the Papacy; the first obviously and explicitly political, the second belonging rather to the general transcendental scheme of Catholicism, but having its political place in the structure of the European world.

Unity through an Empire and a common Imperial idea, the ideal of all Christendom acting under one civil authority in civil matters, had been a reality at the moment when the Græco-Roman Empire accepted the Catholic Faith. It remained an active reality in the Greek East throughout whatever territories were directly administered from Byzantium, and the Emperor in Byzantium was the real ruler of a centralized state.

But in the West, although the conception of Empire remained strong, though men still thought of all political power as ultimately deriving from the Emperor, yet in practice local government superceded the central authority of the universal monarch. We have seen how that local government fell under the control of generals commanding portions of the Roman troops: the federated auxiliary portions largely of German but also of Slav blood, semibarbaric, though Christian and thus part of our civilization.

These local commanders, (the most important of whom by far was the chief ruler in Gaul, who had originally been the commander of the small Frankish contingent of Roman troops), were to be found also in Italy and Spain. In Great Britain, as the Dark Ages advanced, government had almost broken down. There was no one local general nor even three or four arranging affairs between them. Most of the British Bishoprics (the survival of which was a test of civilization) disappeared on the east of the island. But on the Continent, though we were sinking into the Dark Ages, these local governments were strong; and they maintained not only the law courts, but the social traditions and even the coins and currency of the Imperial state. There had been an effort to reëstablish for the West, as a separate unit, an Imperial power of its own. The thing had been done under Charlemagne during that great siege of Christendom of which we have spoken. But the thing did not last. As the Dark Ages proceeded to their lowest depth in the 9th century, after Charlemagne's death and the breakup of his dominions, there was no real Imperial rule left north of South Italy or west of the Adriatic.

Yet the name "Empire" and the idea of Empire survived in the West. It was taken over, oddly enough, by the heads of the newly converted German tribes who claimed through the Imperial name and title the right to exercise authority over North Italy and even in some degree over the districts to the west, of the German speech, the marches between that speech and the Latin speech of Gaul. But by the end of the Middle Ages the word Emperor meant in practice no more than the hereditary house of Hapsburg, ruling its personal domains from Vienna; claiming, but hardly exercising a general authority over the German-speaking divisions, free cities and lesser and greater lordships.

The Papacy survived, of course, far more strongly, but against the Papacy also there had come—indeed it was the essence of the Reformation period—a violent protest and rebellion. As against the political conception of a civil unity under a more or less shadowy Western Emperor there was put forward the theory of the absolute state; each prince, or government of a free city or free canton, supreme in his or its own area.

After the violent religious wars following on the Reformation, the principle was even accepted that the type of religion adopted by the government of each district should rule the spiritual life of all inhabitants thereof.

The acceptance of such an idea confirmed, of course, the political disruption, following on the religious disruption. The effect of this was to permit new civil laws governing social relations, which laws were not subject to the general opinion or the traditions of Christendom. Therefore the new political independent units permitted their rulers to seize the property of what had hitherto been the universal economic structure of the Church.

The monasteries and their wealth could not be touched as long as the Papacy was recognized, for they depended upon the Papacy and not upon the civil power. The same was true of endowments which had been made for the support of secular religion, that is, the revenues of the parish Churches, of the Bishoprics, of the Cathedral Chapters. The same was true of the collegiate revenues, of institutions devoted to education, from the small local schools, every one of which was endowed in such fashion, to the great colleges of the universities. That wealth could not be touched as long as the Papacy was acknowledged. Whenever the authority of the Papacy was denied it lay open to general loot.

Here it is that we see the priority of the political over economic circumstances. Only where the political revolution had been thorough and the government of a district had become supreme, and independent of all external authority, was it possible for that government to seize the goods hitherto under the protection of the Church. And wherever such complete independence prevailed, the clerical goods were seized in whole or in part. The monasteries and nunneries were dissolved. Their wealth was taken wholly away for the benefit of those in power. The endowment of parish Churches, Bishoprics, Chapters, which could not be totally destroyed, lest all forms of corporate religion should cease (and for that men were not prepared), were not wholly confiscated. But they were cut down more and more as time proceeded. The educational endowments went the same way; many ceased altogether to be used for educational purposes, having been grasped by any who had the power to take them and turned to private uses, making of what had been corporate property the personal income of the confiscators. Many more were reëndowed upon a lesser scale, so that the schools went on, though less wealthy than before. The funds of the guilds which were connected with local religious practices were somewhat diminished; and to show how violent was the spirit of rapine, even the endowments of hospitals for the sick largely went the same way.

It is of interest to note how the various parts of Christendom reacted to this political change and its economic consequences. In England, by what was no more than a personal accident the monasteries were seized altogether by the Crown. Within four years of the breach with Rome (that is, of the denial of Papal authority), every monastery and nunnery in England had gone. And all those great revenues—some say a third, but more probably a fifth of the rental surplus values of the country—passed from the hands of the corporate owners, monastic and collegiate, first to the government and very soon to those who were granted the rents on very favorable terms (about half price), from the government in its pressing desire to raise revenue.

The same thing happened though less violently than in England, in Scandinavia and in the northern part of the Low Countries, which were later to be called Holland. In Scotland there was of course a similar confiscation, drastic and universal. Certain of the Swiss cantons had led the movement. Many of the free cities and lesser lords of Germany followed suit. But England was the only considerable political unit which joined in the general seizure of Church revenues.

The greater part of Europe and its chief governments, the Imperial domains in Germany, the French monarchy, the newly consolidated Spanish monarchy with its vast possessions beyond the Atlantic, the Italian States, as they preserved their allegiance to the Papacy, so they preserved the collegiate rights and the monastic establishments, schools, hospitals and the rest. That is, the theory was preserved of clerical endowment. There was in fact a good deal of encroachment even in Catholic times by legal tricks. Nothing had been commoner, for instance, before the loot began, than for the government to make over to some favorite (as for instance a king to an illegitimate son) the revenues of some part of Church endowment, putting in a cleric to do the work of the place, but transferring the bulk of the income to the layman appointed in place of the abbot. Oddly enough England, the one place where the confiscation was most thorough, was also the place where the Church, though corrupt, was at its best; and the monasteries, though they had lost much of their original virtue and at least one-half of their original members, were least encroached upon by laymen. In Scotland this encroachment had been universal and scandalous, and in France almost as bad.

While all this was going on a great deal depended upon the attitude of Calvin. We have seen how Calvin was the major influence giving positive structure and permanence to the new Reformation movement. Calvinism provided the framework of and gave its spirit to this new Protestant world. And as Calvinism was the creation of Calvin, his attitude towards the economic change is of the first importance.

Now that attitude was ambiguous. Although Calvin was the least compromising of men, as direct as he was energetic and creative, he was compelled by the nature of his position and by his very doctrines to unite two contradictory principles.

On the one hand he denied the right of the lay power to immix itself at all in the government of spiritual matters. It should therefore have followed that the lay power could have no opportunity for looting Church property. Church property ought logically, in Calvin's scheme, to have been taken over by his own new counter-church, whenever this prevailed, and should have served for the endowment of activities admitted or created by his new clerical organization. The all-important influence of Calvin and Calvinism ought therefore logically to have worked against the looting of Church property.

But Calvin and his followers were also rooted in another principle and occupied in another activity; the principle that no central authority could be admitted over the Church, on which account Calvinism had attacked the Papacy with special vehemence. Now the power of the Pope alone restrained (as head of the Catholic organization on its spiritual side) that otherwise complete independence which the free cities, the princes, and cantons vehemently affirmed. There remained therefore no alternative for Calvin but to affirm with the utmost clarity and insistence the independence of each civil power. He, more than any other one influence, made secure the new conception of absolute sovereignty, unchecked by the general powers and traditions of Christendom. Hence he it was who let loose an unrestricted power of confiscation and loot over what had been the property of the universal clerical organization of Christendom, although none affirmed more clearly than he the rightful independence of clerical institutions from civil control.

In the upshot, then, the practical influence of Calvin was to make the loot of the Church wherever his influence was felt not only possible, but a matter of course.

When we come to look in more detail at the economic effects of the great change, we find them proceeding from the victory of one philosophy over its opposite.

Under the old social philosophy which had governed the Middle Ages, temporal, and therefore all economic, activities were referred to an eternal standard. The production of wealth, its distribution and exchange were regulated with a view to securing the Christian life of Christian men. In two points especially was this felt: First in securing the independence of the family, which can only be done by the wide distribution of property, in other words the prevention of the growth of a proletariat; secondly, in the close connection between wealth and public function. Under the old philosophy which had governed the high Middle Ages things had been everywhere towards a condition of Society in which property was well distributed throughout the community, and thus the family rendered independent. The slave was slowly becoming the serf, and from the serf, becoming a free peasant. The artisan in the towns, organized in his guild, had control of his own life and that of his family. He was not, as he has now become, the economic subordinate of wealthier men. His relations with his apprentices were organic and domestic, unlike the modern relation of mere mechanical contract between the laborer with the capitalist who exploits him.

That there would be and were large exceptions to all this is manifest; that there were already not a few, though a small minority, who had neither land for tillage nor a house of their own, nor a place in a guild, is true. But these were not numerous enough to give its tone to Society. The society of Christendom and especially of Western Christendom up to the explosion, which we call the Reformation, had been a society of owners: a Proprietarial Society. It was one in which there remained strong bonds between one class and another, and in which there was a hierarchy of superior and inferior, but not, in the main, a distinction between a restricted body of possessors and a main body of destitute at the mercy of the possessors, such as our society has become. It has so become through the action of the Reformation, which was at the root of the whole change.

To begin with, every time a piece of collegiate property such as a monastery, a hospital or a school, was looted, the profits and rents of one man took the place of the livelihood of a whole community. The monks who had formed the units of their society lived on in some places upon pensions, and in others were cast upon the world. But in neither case were they succeeded by another body of corporate owners. In the place of such corporate owners appeared in due time a number of destitute men.

The suppression of the guilds, or, at any rate, their

weakening, worked in the same way. The economic foundations of the guild were shaken by the religious upheaval, because the guild had been inextricably mixed up with religious observance; the Reformation impoverished the guilds, undermined their moral authority and, in the long run, after some generations when its full effect had been felt, the guild dwindled to be a "museum piece": an anachronism, of which the name had been kept, but a totally new function attributed to it. Thus what were once the guilds of the City of London had become by the 19th century dining clubs for rich men, clubs usually endowed with landed and other property. They used many useful functions in the way of education and charities, succoring their impoverished members and dependents, but no longer resembling in any real way the old guilds from which they had sprung. The original Fishmongers' Guild of London regulated the trade in fish, fixed prices, checked undue competition, prevented the wealthier fishmonger from eating up his smaller brother and so on. There is still to this day a Fishmongers' Guild, or Company, as it was and is called, immensely wealthy and giving great banquets in its fine modern hall—the successor of the medieval building destroyed in the Great Fire of London. But it has nothing to do with the trade of fishmongering; it is a mere collection of well-to-do merchants and others who have asked for membership and paid their entrance fee, and thus form the present Fishmongers' Company.*

The Reformation has been called in a biting epigram "a rising of the rich against the poor." Like all epigrams that brief statement is exaggerated, but it contains much

---

* One of the last of the true guilds still performing some shadow of its ancient function was the Innholders, of which the present writer is a member. If he is not mistaken the last active function it exercised, the keeping and regulation of hotels, etc., within the bounds of the City of London, was destroyed by law rather more than a hundred years ago.

more truth than most of its kind. It was from the destruction of the unity of Christendom in the 16th century that there proceeded by various channels those developments which we shall trace in later pages.

Out of them combined came capitalism; the division of Society as a whole into a minority of owners, exploiting a majority of citizens without ownership; the control of industry by organs of credit; the control of those organs of credit by yet smaller numbers of very wealthy men; the powerful and secret organization of such financial control: the increasing insecurity and insufficiency of livelihood among the masses; at last their threat of revolt—and through that threat of revolt the peril now overhanging all our civilization. The Reformation confirmed and in many departments monstrously increased evils already apparent in the later Middle Ages. Status, which had guaranteed a man's livelihood, was replaced by contract. Usury was let loose upon the largest scale until it became universal; competition was allowed to run riot until it covered nearly the whole field of man's actions; banking, based upon usury, and larger and larger commercial units based upon competition, continued the process. By the latter part of the 17th century, when the second lifetime after the catastrophe had matured, men's minds had changed. Central banks were at work. The proletarian spirit had arisen in some districts, notably in England, even upon the land itself, where the peasantry was in process of being destroyed. The greater man was eating up the smaller man in commerce.

When on such a world there came the new machinery and the new rapidity of communications, all social instruments for the checking of capitalist power had been destroyed. That power so grew that by the end of the 18th century capitalism was already in full flood, and became in the 19th century all-powerful. Against it the unfortunate and increasing proletariat was becoming conscious of its misery, groping towards an organization and preparing for revolt. It was inevitable that such an inhuman state of affairs should lead to the catastrophic instability from which we are suffering today.

But why, it may be asked, was there no return? Why was there not a sufficient reaction against dangers so apparent, real and swelling? It was because with the Reformation there had also disappeared not only in the societies which broke away from Christian unity, but in the others as well, the old mental attitude called "Faith." By this is not meant that *the* Faith disappeared—that is, the acceptation of the authority and doctrines of the Catholic Church.

Manifestly this did not disappear, save under governments which had broken with the unity of Christendom; and even under these governments large bodies of citizens remained fighting a rearguard action (as in England and Holland) and maintaining for generations a dwindling minority of Catholic resistance. Neither does it mean that all the prime doctrines which a united Christendom had held were abandoned in the Protestant areas. On the contrary, certain of the old doctrines were still almost universally held, for instance, that of the Incarnation and the Trinity. Others were still virtually held by the whole of Christian doctrine, such as the immortality of the soul and the eternity of blessedness and its opposite after death. The quality of Faith, which may be defined as certitude in things not demonstrable by direct experience or deductive proof, remained. But it remained in isolated groups; it did not remain as a universal habit native to all men of our blood, taken for granted, and ruling their lives.

Because there had arisen such permanent diversity in the morals affirmed in the doctrinal statements on which those morals were founded, there had arisen at the same time an underlying, unexpressed feeling that life could not be conducted upon any general norm common to the whole of our civilization. There was no longer One Society bound by one moral bond, represented by one moral head, expressing itself in one liturgy and able as only a personality can, to react against that which threatened its existence. Local resistance there would be, as against the break-up of the family through divorce, as against excessive competition, etc.; though it was kept up with dwindling energy. It was so kept up, of course, longer in the Catholic sections of Europe than in the non-Catholic, but everywhere the whole Society of Christendom was infected by this loss of unity, producing as its inevitable fruit the loss of all capacity for coördinated resistance to the growing spiritual evils now upon it.

Those spiritual evils, working in alliance with a vastly expanding knowledge of the material world, could not in the long run, but destroy the health of Europe. Men were blind to the consequences, even those living in the healthier parts of Christendom, which remained Catholic. They were not awake to the forces which would produce their necessary consequences. Today the consequences are upon us, the whole structure of life is in peril of immediate ruin.

Here we leave the statement of the great upheaval and its immediate consequences, economic and political. We turn next to those separate developments as proceeding from the break-up of unity—the effect of unchecked greed through Usury, through the mechanization of life, and the rest. We shall see how, under the intolerable strain, a Social Revolution was at first confusedly proposed and at last definitely formulated, and how the final fruit of the affair, today called Communism, matured.

IV

THE ULTIMATE CONSEQUENCES
OF THE REFORMATION

(a) GROWTH OF THE PROLETARIAT
AND CAPITALISM

Contract Replaces Status

HITHERTO WE HAVE followed the founding and development of our civilization, its high moment in the true
Middle Ages; the peril it ran at the end of the Middle
Ages, and the final crash of the Reformation, in which
for a moment all appeared lost.

We have also followed the more immediate results
of that catastrophe, particularly of the loot of the Church
and the inroads made upon communal and corporate life.

So far also we have followed the process more or less
historically; that is, consecutively from the old pagan days
through the conversion and the formation of Christendom
to its violent disruption at the end of 1500 years.

Now we turn to another method. We shall follow each
development of the catastrophe separately, showing how
one element after another went on its way reacting on
and reacted upon by other developments side by side with
it. We shall trace, one after the other, the main tendencies

133

flowing from the original breakdown, and show how at last they had converged into the present perilous situation which I have called "The Crisis of Civilization." Only when we shall have followed each of these tendencies produced by the Reformation shall we turn to the last section and consider the possible remedy for evils now upon us.

For the Reformation as a catastrophe I have used the metaphor of an explosion. I spoke of its immediate results as one would speak after an explosion of the clouds and smoke and dust, the ruins, the roar, and the rest. Thus I emphasized the loot of the Church, the breakdown of any common international authority and standard for keeping Christendom together, the huge wars which were let loose, and, in the loss of unity, loss of faith.

Now that we come to the slow and ultimate results, we must change the metaphor and I compare the matter no longer to an explosion but rather to the breaking down of a dam which restrains a great head of water. The metaphor is just, for before the Reformation broke out there had accumulated a strain just like a head of water of increasing pressure, against which artificial restraint would sooner or later prove useless. The dam broke, the flood poured tumultuously over all the lower lands. After the first chaos of swirling torrent and deeply flooded land, the waters begin to take particular channels; they wander by diverse ways through the countryside below the place where the original dam stood; at last they tend to converge, they form a new accumulation. Once more tension arises, once more the danger of catastrophe is apparent. But there is this difference between the catastrophe of which we now stand in peril and the catastrophe of the Reformation. After the Reformation our civilization survived, indeed its technical performances increased. Its spiritual loss was disastrous and was bound to produce at last what it has produced—the danger of death for the whole. But in the material world, what followed on the catastrophe was at first a continual and at last a rapid expansion and advance. This was particularly so in the field of physical science and the discovery of the earth. But today what threatens us through the loss of religion is the total collapse of Society and with it the corresponding loss of all the arts and sciences—the end of our civilization.

These ultimate results of the Reformation, these streams of tendency which we can follow down, each in its own channel separately, from that one source, "the bursting of the dam," I shall treat of under the following heads:

First, the replacement of Status by Contract. This must come at the beginning because it formed the general condition under which all the rest was possible. It was because Status decayed and Contract took its place that all the modern development, up to these last dangerous moments of ours today, was capable of appearing. The growth of Contract replacing Status was not a cause of the evils that followed, but it was a condition without which they could not have come about.

After a survey of this main change, I shall consider the twin results of newly invigorated greed: first Usury and then Competition.

Next we will turn to the rise of a proletariat—an inevitable result of Competition in the absence of Status. After that we will turn to the new commerce and banking, then to the effect of machines, which greatly expanded, and at the same time degraded, the laboring population.

After that we shall see the first protest arising against conditions that were gradually becoming intolerable. We shall follow the rise of various theories of Socialism, which were the voice of that protest; we shall see how Socialism gathers, and lastly how, in the maturity of all this, we get the fully defined, most powerful and active affair called Communism.

Communism, the ultimate fruit of the Reformation, is clearly the mortal enemy of all that by which we have lived and by which our culture continues. Its victory would be our death.

Having postulated the menace of Communism we shall consider what remedies can be proposed as an alternative to the false remedy which Communism offers.

In all this a warning is necessary, which is that what the Reformation did was not to create the seeds of all those evils from which we now suffer. Every one of the features we are now about to consider—the growth of Contract at the expense of Status, the presence of Usury and of Competition, the power of commerce and of banking, the effect of machines—all these can be discovered in some degree of growth present among us long before the Reformation period. Some of them have always been present in human society and in the nature of things always will be.

No, the novel effect of the Reformation was not the starting or creating of any of these things but a change in *degree*.

Remember that it is by degree all things are characterized. The difference between a caress and a deadly blow is only a difference of degree. The difference between the slight and genial exhilaration of a good meal with moderate drink and the bestial and destructive thing called drunkenness is only a question of degree. The difference between reticence or even slight eccentricity, and madness is only a difference of degree. It was not the mere presence of even such an evil as usury which appeared as a novelty after the Reformation. It was rather the running riot of that evil. It was not the presence of a certain number of landless men and of the destitute—that is, of a proletariat —which was novel after the Reformation, it was the growth of such numbers of these that they became the great mass of certain communities. It was not the hardship of life produced by poverty which was proper to the Reformation, it was a hardness of conditions grown to an intolerable weight; insufficiency and insecurity of industrialized masses goading them to frenzy.

All this being said, let us see how Contract began to eat up Status.

First of all, what is "status"? The meaning of the word is "standing." The status of a man is his established condition. In our original Christian society—that society which reached its flower in the Middle Ages—status was omnipresent. It did not cover the whole ground of human activity by any means, but it covered a sufficient area to make status the determining character of all our society. A man's position was known, the duties and burdens attaching to it were known, as also the advantages, and they were in a large measure fixed; for the spiritual force and motive underlying the whole business was an appetite for security: for making life tolerable on its material side so that there should be room and opportunity for men to lead the good life, as the Greeks put it, or, as the Catholic Church puts it, to save their souls.

Status arose from the strong, instinctive demand of a Catholic society for stable social relations between men, and, what was much more important, for a stable sufficiency of livelihood attaching to the great mass of families in the community. With the loss of religion Status has almost wholly disappeared today, and nowhere more than in the most advanced communities. Its disappearance is particularly striking among yourselves here in America. Under Status one man was the accepted superior of another or again one man had a function attached to him which was admitted and permanent and which distinguished him from the function of another man. The artisan was in the scheme of Society below the lord of a village, but he had full standing as a member of his guild. The serf, who later became the peasant in the village, was even lower than the artisan in the social scale, but he was certain of his position, he had an hereditary holding, and could not be rendered landless or destitute. He had Status. Status governed the whole arrangements of the Church, of course, but also the main arrangements of civil society. Today there survives of it in particular the status of offices in the Catholic Church and certain vague and insecure definitions in other activities. In some of the professions there is still a large element of status, notably in the law and in medicine, still more in the armed services of the State.

Indeed, Status is so necessary to the nature of man, in some degree at least, that it can never die out, but, in so far as it can die out, it had died out in the last phase of modern times. Even when Status was at its highest, Contract was present. It was present whenever one man made a purchase of anything from another man in a market. It was present whenever man bargained even for an extension or development of Status itself. There had always been contract in the matter of merchandise, though restricted by the guild system, and there was contract in a hundred details of daily life.

Towards the end of the Middle Ages, long before Contract grew to be so important as to eat up Status, there were arising new conditions which would favor Contract as against Status.

There was the study of Roman Law, which gradually

modified and began to oust the traditional popular law of the Middle Ages. The Roman Law gave sanction to contract, not custom. Man under Roman Law, which was rediscovered in the Middle Ages, did not hold his land feudally as an inherited right; he held it by purchase or by a will; he was an owner, an absolute owner; and the whole point of ownership was the right to contract and the duty enforceable by the State of fulfilling a contract. Apart from Roman Law, which was the first influence beginning to make Contract encroach upon Status, was the growth of oversea trade with geographic expansion. You could restrict the profits which an individual tried to acquire by special contracts with his neighbors, but you could not restrict the contracts which made the oversea merchant wealthy, for your corporate society had no jurisdiction over the provider of foreign goods.

Then again, as the serf began to merge into the peasant, Contract began to destroy Status. When the guild flourished it was ruled by the conception of the just price and the same idea of the guild worked through village life by making tenure of land fixed and hereditary. But when the guild decayed as a result of the Reformation, when controlled industry proved unable to compete with competitive industry, Contract rapidly took the place of Status. In the case of the peasant—that is, of the small, landed man—a double process took place, which was the more important cause. Until comparatively recent times, the tillers of the land formed the vast majority of the people of Christendom. In this double process, the peasant tended to fall to the state of a mere laborer as in England, so that he lost Status altogether and had no bond with any one save by Contract; he had not even the right to remain alive. While on the other side, as for instance in France, the peasant, by becoming completely independent of local rules and of a lord, also got rid of Status, and his functions became purely functions of Contract.

At last there came in an even more powerful influence for the destruction of Status. That was the increasing mobility of fortune. In the days of Status, the great family was one that had been wealthy for a long time. Men reposed in the idea that such wealth was permanent, and, with the passage of the generations, such wealth naturally bred respect. It had a status of its own. For wealth has a mystical effect even when it is mere temporary possession, and that effect is vastly enhanced when the possession stretches over a long space of time. But when wealth was mobilized, when it became (to use another metaphor) liquid, all that changed. A family very wealthy in one generation and ruined in the next gives no impression of Status. Men came at last to consider only the momentary position and to give it no particular respect. They could envy it and they could hate it, but they could not revere it.

With all these influences increasing throughout three hundred years and becoming riotous today—that is, increasing feverishly—we come to the end of a process whereby in the loss of Status and the replacement of it by Contract we have found chaos; a society without bond or cement. We have further produced an economic state of affairs in which the condition of the mass of men deprived of Status is desperate. That is why in their persistent efforts to reëstablish security and sufficiency for themselves, the modern proletariat is really expressing and apparently beginning to satisfy an appetite for Status.

Usury and Competition

Two further consequences following on the destruction of moral unity in Europe appear in our examination of the road by which we came to the pass in which we now find ourselves. These two are the direct fruits of unchecked greed: greed working without the restraint which had been put upon its action by the moral code of the Catholic centuries, but which, once there was no central authority at work, could do its utmost unchecked.

These two primary fruits of greed were Usury and Unlimited Competition.

Through Usury there arose that simplification and consequent centralization of credit-control which was to be so powerful an instrument in the hands of the class newly enriched by the loot of the Reformation; which Competition, no longer checked by the guild, by customary Catholic morals and by the Catholic inspiration of Society, was inevitably to produce that proletariat, whose complaint at the injustice of their condition has ended in the menace to civilization now before us.

Competition working on a society which had lost the idea of Status and had replaced it by the idea of Contract, was to ruin the multitude of small owners and to produce increasing masses of men subject to the mere power of wealth, without a human bond between them and their new masters. This power of wealth was to be accentuated through the centralized control of credit, a product of unchecked Usury. The proletariat so created became a larger and larger part of Society, while their masters, the capitalist owners of the means of production, became a smaller and smaller part of Society, under the rise of the new international commerce and of banking. This development of Capitalism was to be later accentuated by a new rapidity of communication and the extended use of machinery.

At the end of the process conditions were becoming intolerable for the mass of wage-earners who had formerly been economically free men but who were now half slaves. Protest began, which was at first confusedly expressed in various forms of Socialist theory. These various reactions of the exploited against the exploiters matured and gradually coalesced into full Communism, which today proposes by a simple formula the emancipation of the wage-slaves, but only to their own destruction and at the same time the destruction of our religion and civilization. Such is the chain of cause and effect we are now about to follow.

Usury, to take that first, like the greed from which it proceeds, is as old as human society. Like the other evils proceeding from the Reformation it was not created by the movement. We shall find in the case of Usury, as in the case of unbridled Competition, (the force which, coupled with Usury, achieved the creation and enslavement of the proletariat), as likewise we have already found in the case of Contract replacing Status, that the seeds of the change had been sown long before the actual disruption of Christendom took place. What happened after the Reformation was not that these new evils, including Usury, then appeared for this first time but, as I have said, that they turned from exceptions into admitted and general habits. They were accepted, they grew, and at last came to cover the whole field of Society.

Unlike the transformation of Status into Contract and the undue growth of Competition, Usury was an evil in itself.

It was not only evil because it got out of proportion, and swelled beyond due measure, as did the replacement of Status by Contract and the practice of Competition, but was of its own nature a thing to be condemned and extirpated, if possible, as a disease. It may be remarked that it had already permeated like a mortal poison the society of pagan antiquity at its close and was one of the main evils under which the society of Græco-Roman civilization collapsed in the West, and before the Mahommedan invasion in the East.*

The morals of the Church, when the Church gradually overcame the world and moulded a new Europe, forbade Usury as strongly, though not with so much practical effect, as did later Mahommedanism. Every sane philosophy, every religion, had forbidden it. The Greek pagan philosophers with Aristotle at their head denounced it; so did the Oriental pagans; so did the Jewish law.

Now why was this? Why was Usury thus regarded universally as immoral, and why has it been found in practice to be a poison ultimately destroying Society?

In order to answer these questions we must first understand what Usury is, in the sense in which we here employ the term; for there is great ambiguity in the use of the word and therefore misunderstanding of the thing which the word connotes.

Usury in the sense of an economic evil does not mean the taking of interest on a loan. It does not mean the taking of interest higher than some permitted minimum. It means the taking of interest upon a loan of *money alone* (or still worse, upon a mere promise to lend money, an instrument of credit) whether that money be invested soundly or no, whether it represent productive energy or no. Usury is, properly speaking, the taking of increment upon a loan of money *merely because it is money* or worse

---

* It must be remarked that one of the principal factors of success in the Mahommedan over-running of half Christendom between the 7th and 8th centuries was its active penalizing of Usury. This leading tenet of Islam in its social morals gave immediate relief to myriads of debtors in North Africa, Syria, and Mesopotamia. It is strictly enforced today. Nothing is more remarkable in the Mahommedan countries of North Africa today than to see how, under the rule of Europeans there, the Mahommedan still refuses to take interest from his fellow Mahommedan on a mere loan of money, and how the whole trade of Usury is confined to the European immigrants and the native Jews.

still the taking of such increment upon a credit-instrument.

The reasons for condemning interest upon money alone, as distinguished from profit, are twofold: First, it is asking a tribute from Society as the price of releasing currency hitherto withheld from its proper function of acting as the circulating medium of exchange; secondly it is arranging a claim for payment of a share in profit which may, *but also may not,* exist.

As an example of the first evil, let us consider a market in which the supply of currency is in the hands of a small number of those present, buyers and sellers; or even in an extreme case (the case of many a bank in a small market town) in the hands of one controller only.

No transactions in the market, save those of mere barter, can take place unless the monopolist holding the currency permit it to be used for its natural purpose.

The natural purpose of currency is this: the facilitation of the multiple exchange of goods. If I have a surplus of wheat, having produced more than I can consume of that article, while my neighbor has a surplus of hay, having produced more than his establishment can consume, we will, if we are in contact, naturally exchange the hay for the wheat; since it is to the mutual advantage of both of us that we should do so.

Now let us suppose a third party, who had produced more potatoes than he can consume, but has not sufficient hay for his purpose; a fourth who has livestock for food in excess of his needs and would exchange the surplus for wheat; a fifth who is a craftsman and has produced clothes and boots for the supply of others in exchange for goods which he needs. Then there arises a condition not of simple barter but of *multiple exchange.*

The man with the hay is not in contact with the man who produced boots, nor either of them with the man who has a surplus of potatoes. There must be present a common medium of exchange which shall circulate among them if the various surpluses are to be distributed according to the demands of the producers and purchasers.

That is the true function of money, and of instruments of credit based upon money: to make possible the action of multiple exchange.

Now in so far as the monopolists hold back this current medium from general circulation, demanding a price for its use, they are demanding increment for something which has no natural increment: which does not breed. They are asking for a surplus although that which they advance produces of itself no surplus. They are holding up the community by refusing it its normal medium of exchange.

That is the first wrong attaching to taking interest upon money alone. The second—and in complex times such as ours, much the most important—evil attaching to usury is the *taking of increment from a non-productive loan.*

This is manifestly immoral.

A man comes to me and says: "I have found upon my property a vein of ore, but it lies deep, so that I shall require a considerable capital—say $100,000.—to extract the valuable metal. That metal, when it shall have been extracted, will be worth at least $200,000. But I cannot obtain this advantage until I purchase the instruments for developing the mine and have hired the labor required to work it. Lend me the $100,000. necessary for the operation." I answer him: "If I do so, you must give me a share in the profit, say, half the total." He agrees that without my capital he could not develop the mine; without his ore my capital would not be used. The combination of the two is productive of wealth, and we share that wealth. That is a perfectly moral transaction, even if the profit be one of 100 percent or 1000 percent over the original investment; so that, with my stipulated half profit, I make 50 percent or 500 percent on my original loan, I am in no way to blame. The increment is not properly speaking interest on a loan of money; it is a share of real wealth.

But if I lend the money, saying; "I care not what your profits may be, nor whether there be a profit or no, but I demand $10,000. a year for the use of my $100,000."— then in case the speculation fails the borrower will be bound to pay the $10,000. perpetually, without any production of wealth to correspond to it. He will then be paying interest on an unproductive loan, and it is manifestly immoral to ask for share of wealth which does not exist.

Now any loan at interest which is a loan of mere money *may* partake of this character; and among a number of such loans many will partake of this unproductive character. Of the money bearing interest merely because it is money, some large proportion at any one time must be demanding interest from activities which create no wealth out of which to pay the interest.

For instance, nearly all the War Loans issued in the belligerent countries to pay for the Great War were loans unproductive of wealth, yet bearing interest. The money was expended, not in developing productive capacity, not in turning potential wealth into actual wealth, but in feeding men occupied in killing each other, in clothing them, in giving them their wages, and armament. When the effort was over, a vast indebtedness remained; a vast annual interest was claimed in perpetuity—and yet there had been no wealth produced out of which such increment could come.

But though Usury is in itself immoral, and justly condemned by every moral code, its chief and worst defect in the particular case we are now examining, the growth of Capitalism and its increasing proletariat, is the centralization of irresponsible control over the lives of men: the putting of power over the proletariat into the hands of a few who can direct the loans of currency and credit without which that proletariat could not be fed and clothed and maintained in work.

It is manifestly easier to make a merger in mere paper interests, in the mere bookkeeping of bankers, than it is to make a merger of activities in real things.

One set of capitalists control a particular railway, having certain problems to solve, and certain public needs to serve. Another set control another railway, and have another and different set of conditions to meet and different needs to serve. It may be difficult to adjust the functions of the two so that both shall come under one control, though such a combination promises advantages through the lessening of expense in management. But the merger of two financial groups can be, as it were, automatic. There is no material obstacle. You are but arranging a profitable combination in the common art of book-keeping. Therefore Usury, that is, the taking of interest on an advance of money or credit alone without consideration of whether actual wealth shall be produced or no, tends to centralize. You get in the long run a sort of octopus which throws its tentacles over the whole of Society. The institutions of credit become the normal depositories of innumerable private credits, and of collections of currency, whence they base further credits. Loans both for production and for activities which will produce nothing, many such loans so issuing from one source, all of them bearing interest, and therefore some part of them bearing interest on non-productive investment —that is making a claim for wealth which is not really there—impoverish and deliberately destroy the debtor by putting him under tribute to pay, though he has no source of income produced by the sum which he borrowed. The most familiar instance is the ruin of a farmer through foreclosure on his mortgage by a bank.

Usury so extended throughout a community, so taken for granted, lays the community under an unjust tribute and at the same time becomes the central controller, whether through productive or unproductive loans, of most social activities.

The larger the unit of capital present, the easier the transaction called emission of credit. Centralized lending of this kind (which is today universal) actively promotes the absorption of the small man by the great, the reduction of small property owners to a proletarian condition.

It is with Usury as with other evils in Society, apart from its original immorality and the manifest causes thereof: it produces secondary effects which are also evil, until it has infected the whole community.

As long as Usury was forbidden by the moral law and its immorality admitted, even though it took place widely, it took place under protest. It was always checked by the public disrepute in which it was held and by the fact that unless it were disguised, the interest could not be recovered by law. Disguises were indeed often used, as for instance, the promise to repay on a certain date a certain sum of money as having been lent, when as a fact a small sum had been lent. But though such subterfuges were continual, the evil could not spread until the taking of interest upon money alone became an admitted practice of which no man was ashamed, which no one thought evil, which was taken for granted.

That is precisely what happened within the space of about two lifetimes after the Reformation first broke down our common morals. By the third generation great central banks had arisen, notably in Amsterdam and London. Shortly afterwards, during the 18th century, men had everywhere begun to think (later in Catholic societies than in Protestant, but everywhere at last) as though interest on money were part of the nature of things: as though money had indeed, merely *as* money, a right to breed. The false doctrine was bound to lead to a deadlock at last, and in our own time that deadlock had been reached. The recovery of the vast usurious loans is becoming impossible. Recourse has had to be made to repudiation on all sides and the whole system is breaking down.

But remember that the worst of its effects is not its own self-destruction, but the way in which it has gathered into a few centers the power of controlling the lives of the community and particularly of the proletariat, whose employment and therefore existence, depends upon the advance of credit by the holders of financial power. For all our great enterprises today are possible only through the favor of the lenders of money or credit.

We may sum up then and say that the unrestricted admittance of Usury as a normal economic function about a lifetime after the Reformation advanced the destruction of economic freedom, the swallowing up of the small man by the greater man, and the ultimate production of a large destitute Proletariat in the following fashions:

(1) By the eating up of small property by Usury, falling as it did habitually upon men already embarrassed, and achieving their ruin;

(2) By transferring real wealth in goods and land to those who directly used their mere money power, often enormous and impersonal, through mortgage and foreclosure.

The second of the two forces let loose by the Reformation for the ultimate destruction of economic freedom and the production of Capitalism with its now revolutionary proletariat was the force of Unrestricted Competition.

Here we must be careful to note again that, unlike Usury, competition is an evil only as it passes beyond certain limits. Usury is an evil always and everywhere. It is a moral evil in itself and of evil social effect by its very nature. To take interest on money without considering on what the money is spent, necessarily involves the taking of profit on an unproductive loan; means recurrent ruin of some among the borrowers perpetually.

But competition is in the very nature of Society. The moment a community begins to create wealth according to the aptitudes of each producer and to exchange the wealth so created, competition must necessarily appear. There was plenty of competition in the centuries during which Catholic principles were universally applied to Society; there was plenty of haggling and arrangement of prices by buyer and seller in the medieval markets. The very idea of "a just price," which was at the foundation of all medieval social economics, involves the idea of a price arrived at by some form of competitive activity; for if there were no competition, no price could be settled, or even arrived at.

It is with competition as it is with a thousand other things: up to a certain point they are at once necessary and beneficent; exaggerated beyond that point they begin to be perilous; still further exaggerated they become poisonous and mortal.

Now competition begins to bear this vicious character destructive of Society through the destruction of the small man, when it is uncorrected by the conception of a guild and coöperative rules and of supervision watching for, and checking, economic action destructive of the small owner.

So long as Status rules Society and Contract is only

in part admitted, Competition is thereby necessarily checked. A man who was a member of a village community in Catholic times could get such and such a price for his wheat by competition in the open market; a craftsman would get such and such a price for the object he had made, and the more efficient craftsmen would naturally get more than the less efficient. The more industrious in domestic commerce (foreign commerce was largely free from supervision) would accumulate wealth more rapidly than the less industrious. But all through that world there vigorously existed regulations jealously guarding the division of property among many families and preventing the great man from eating up the small.

The craftsman of the town guild could not form a monopoly; he could not undertake more than a certain amount of work to the detriment of his fellow craftsmen. The same was true of the shopkeeper, whose activities were regulated, or at least limited, by the Company or Guild of which he formed a member. The number of apprentices he might take was subject to license; and the prices he might charge lay between certain known limits. He might not forestall. He might not speculate. Still less might he temporarily sell at a loss and so ruin a competitor artificially.

The maleficent activity of excessive competition, of Competition unchecked and uncontrolled, was prevented, because it was regarded as a disease in Society (which indeed it is) and treated as a disease mortal to human dignity and freedom; just as we regard grave excesses in drink—though fermented liquor in moderation is natural and does no harm. We have unfortunately in the modern world only too much experience of what unbridled competition will do; there are few who have not come across one or another of its evil effects. But we shall judge them more clearly if we tabulate them here in their order.

I say that the small man is dispossessed progressively; his economic freedom destroyed and "eaten up," as the phrase goes, by the larger man, if Competition be unlimited. Now the consideration of the following points will make this evident. There are seven main ways in which Unrestricted Competition destroys the small owner.

(1) The greater part of what are called "overhead charges," the cost of management and the details of furnishing and instrumentation and numerous other details of commercial productive activity, is less, in proportion to the concentration of capital. Ten small shops cost more to run all put together than one large shop ten times the size of each small unit. Moreover the management of a large unit being less human and less domestic than that of a small unit, its discipline can be more rigorously maintained and all manner of economies effected by eliminating human feelings, which would have to be taken into consideration by the owner of a smaller unit. Great factories, great departments, chain store organizations, everything of that kind, run with the precision of a machine and what may be called (if we eliminate the human factor) the "efficiency" of the machine. Therefore, in Competition, the large unit can outdo the smaller unit and does in practice destroy the small unit, as we see happening today upon every side.

(2) The large unit, especially the individual controlling large capital—the large manager or the large owner—is in a better position for receiving information than his smaller rival.

We had in England after the Great War an excellent example of this. The great landowners being—or, at any rate, their advisers being—of a class with special powers for obtaining international knowledge, could safely predict that the high agricultural prices, consequent upon the dearth which necessarily followed the conflict, would not last for long. Men's powers of productivity had been enhanced during the period of the War by the stimulus which had been given to scientific discovery and the creation of new machines, and there was bound to come a glut of produce in agriculture as in everything else.

But the small man had not the same opportunity for judging the immediate future as the big man had. When the landlords offered to sell the land to their tenant farmers, the farmers eagerly bought because they imagined that high prices of agricultural produce had come to stay. They had not the money indeed to buy the farms for themselves, but they could and did borrow the purchase price at usury from the banks. When the fall in prices came, they could with difficulty keep up their payments; for the profits out of which payments should have come had disappeared. The effect of the whole transaction was that masses of English land had been transferred from the old great Landlords to the banks, and that the men who actually tilled the soil and had adventured their small capital in the deveopment of small farms, were left paying tribute to the money-lending machine which modern banking has become.

That is only one instance; many others will occur to the reader within his own experience. Everywhere the large man (though he often ruins himself by speculation) is, other things being equal, in a better position to judge the market than the small man, and from this second cause the large unit, if Competition be unchecked, eats up the lesser.

(3) The third avenue whereby this evil increases is the superiority the large man has in the way of publicity. It is notorious that money spent upon advertising in any form, whether straightforwardly or by secret commissions and bribery, is more effective, out of all proportion, as the scale of payment increases. A hundred thousand dollars

a year spent in advertising some particular goods will have far more than ten times the effect on sales than an expenditure of ten thousand dollars. The expenditure of a million dollars will have far more than ten times the effect on sales than an expenditure of a hundred thousand dollars. Through this command of publicity the large man can, once more, outdistance and destroy the competition of the small man. Further, as his scale increases he can exercise greater pressure upon the organs of publicity; he is more necessary to the newspaper owners than is his humbler rival, and attains thereby further indirect publicity over and above the direct publicity of the advertisement.

(4) The same is true of the power of secrecy purchasable by large units of capital. They are far more effective in this disreputable form of activity (and it is as universal as it is disreputable) than are the lesser men. An excellent example of this evil is to be seen in the patent medicine trade. That trade is almost wholly charlatan. A right to monopoly in some simple remedy is purchased from the public authorities. The remedy is then sold under a fancy name and a price put upon it producing huge profits, all of which are dependent upon the duping of the public. The whole thing would be blown sky-high if the ingredients of the patent medicines and other concoctions were given in plain language and in full, and if their wholesale price were also published. Mr. Orage, one of the most active and intelligent reformers of the last generation in England, attempted this very necessary thing. He, in his little intellectual review which was supported by so brilliant a group of writers for so many years, published week after week the ingredients of the English patent medicines and the cost of those ingredients. Not a single one of the newspapers followed suit, or dared publish so much as the fact that Orage was thus

acting courageously in his own limited sphere for the public good.

That is an example of comparatively simple and innocuous secrecy. In the purchase of silence on much more dangerous lines, large capital is of course supreme and small capital would at once be prosecuted as a matter of course. Large capital can build up legal costs by appeal, whereas small capital will have exhausted its resources long before the final court is reached.

(5) It is equally clear that large units of capital will be tempted to accumulate by the hope of lesser increments than will small units of capital. To add another ten thousand dollars to your original capital of ten thousand dollars involves severe self-restraint and perpetual foregoing of immediate pleasure or even necessity for the sake of accumulation. But the business with a million dollars capital will accumulate a further million dollars at the same percentage of reward without any strain upon the men who control these large masses of capital. There is no personal self-sacrifice involved; there is no abstention from any luxury. In other words the first steps in the accumulation of capital are indefinitely harder than the next, and the last steps in the accumulation of capital, the steps taken by the major units, so far from being difficult, come, as it were, automatically. After a certain stage of growth the difficulty is not to increase the unit, but to prevent its swelling.

(6) As with the growth of capital, so with access to credit. The smaller man approaching our modern banking system, which controls all issue of credit and therefore pretty well all our industrial and commercial activities, is not what the controllers of that credit call "interesting." He borrows with difficulty and upon high terms, and must pledge security out of all proportion to that which his richer rival has to put down. The very large units of

production and exchange have access to credit on a large scale, sometimes without any cover at all, merely upon the prospect of their success, and always upon terms far easier than are open to their smaller rivals. It is perhaps on this line of easier credit that large capital today does most harm to small capital, drives it out and ruins it.

(7) But the worst, morally, and most destructive in practice, of all the functions whereby large capital destroys small ownership is the power and use of underselling. It is a grossly immoral act and one which in all sane societies has been severely punished—but in the competitive society of today it is taken for granted. The small man cannot stand the loss to which the large man challenges him during the struggle between them; he is ruined where his rival survives.

In general, under competition unchecked by coöperative rules and the spirit of the guild or by usage having the force of law and restraining the eating up of the small man by the great, that murderous process takes place inevitably, and, as it were, automatically. Now the man who was once a small owner and is now dispossessed, becomes proletarian.

To give but one example out of fifty, where there were, in my own country, many thousands of grocers with individual shops, men economically free, dependent upon their own efforts and servants to none, there are now as many thousands who are mere managers for a great combine or trust, a thing without personal conscience or responsibility, a bitterly hard master and yet one upon whose goodwill the very lives of all these men who were once independent now hang. I can remember the day when they were economically free. I have lived into a day when they are, to repeat the vigorous metaphor of the Marxians, wage-slaves.

Coupled with Usury, Unrestricted Competition destroys

the small man for the profit of the great and in so doing produces that mass of economically unfree citizens whose very political freedom comes in question because it has no foundation in any economic freedom, that is, any useful proportion of property to support it. Political freedom without economic freedom is almost worthless, and it is because the modern proletariat has the one kind of freedom without the other that its rebellion is now threatening the very structure of the modern world.

Machinery and Rapid Communications

While the growth of banking and international commerce riveted the capitalist system more securely upon Society, another process was developing, which came in to add to the effect of the international mercantile spirit and the international financial organization. This was the growth of machinery and of rapid intercommunication.

We must define our terms:

"Machinery" has always been used in the sense of secondary mechanical appliances. When first a man took a piece of timber and used it as a lever to prize up a stone, he was indeed using a mechanical appliance—that is, some instrument other than that of his own limbs. But he was using it directly. When, very much later, he began to use a second lever in order to increase the power of the first, he had initiated machinery—that is, a use of secondary appliances removed one degree further from the primitive use of the human limb, to do his work. When man used any kind of natural fan, such as a palm leaf, to make a local draft that should blow the chaff away from the wheat, his work was only one step removed from the still simpler method of blowing into it with his mouth. But when he attached a number of vanes to a wheel, and thus produced a permanent wind for the winnowing of the wheat, without the direct intervention of his hand, through an intermediate instrument, he was using a machine.

Now the original machines that man thus devised for himself were not of their nature expensive. They might become expensive through the scale upon which they were made, but they were not expensive in principle. Even so complicated a piece of machinery as a windmill was something that a man could set up in simple form for a few hundred dollars. It was when men began to devise machines on quite another scale that the machine came in to support and extend Capitalism among mankind: when the ordinary small owner, or even somewhat larger owner, could not hope to purchase the machine himself out of his private means.

The main cause of this revolution, the appearance of large-scale machinery, was the perfection and bringing into use of the steam engine, though before this there had already been harnessed on a fairly large scale the power of falling water. It is from this last that we get the term "mill" applied to a factory. In Lancashire, in England today, we talk of cotton mills—a term dating from the time when the machinery of the mills was driven by water. This also explains the geographical situation of the early English machine "concentrations," (ironically called today "manufactories," as though men were still making things in them by hand!) in the valleys of rapid streams.

Let us here point out in passing a matter to which we shall return more than once and which has already been touched upon when we were considering the organization of industry in Catholic times. Had there been any existent vital and energetic institution left in Society after the Reformation for the use of small property in coördinated form—that is, in combination, so that the average man's holding could be put to useful purpose in company with the holdings of a great number of other men of his own sort, the new evils would not have arisen.

There were instruments in use in the old days, as, for instance, in building a harbor. The big instruments would drive in piles in the setting up of cities (such as Venice) upon swampy land, which were quite beyond the means of the master-mason or master-carpenter of the day. But the guild could and did undertake the common work and share out the benefices of the wealth it produced. The guild watched jealously against the encroachments of the contractor; indeed it usually eliminated the necessity of that intermediary altogether, and it watched still more jealously over the continued possession by the small man of his grip upon the means of production.

But the guild and all the spirit of the guild had been destroyed in the great religious catastrophe of the 16th century: that destruction having been completed in the 17th and early 18th. When large concentrated machinery came in the middle and later 18th century and was combined with the use of large-scale credit from the new banking system, small men were quite out of touch with the innovation. They could not, save in combination, purchase the new instrument or make the buildings for accommodating them. But their power of combination had been destroyed together with the force of a combined social religion in which the power of combination had been rooted.

This does not mean that individual small men could not become big capitalists under the new system. They certainly could do so by a mixture of talent, foresight, secrecy, industry, and, above all, greed. All of which characters you find combined, for instance, in such a man as Arkwright, who made his huge fortune out of a new spinning machine. But the fact that the individual could take advantage of the new conditions to outstrip individuals of his own type and become their economic master, while they drifted into wage-slavery under him, makes no exception to the rule that big machinery reinforced Capitalism. On the contrary, it proves the case against big machinery as nothing else could prove it. When it is objected that under the new system the small man could rise, and that, therefore, no social injustice was done, an elementary truth is obscured or implicitly denied—to wit, the elementary truth that the well-being of one man, risen over, and so destroying a multitude of his fellows by competition, is the exact opposite of the well-being of all men.

Anyhow, it is manifest that the discovery and use of these new great instruments strengthened, made permanent, and (unless the philosophy of Society were changed) inevitable, the Capitalist development.

This development had for its original home and breeding-ground industrial Protestant England and the industrial Protestant lowlands of Scotland. From these the influence spread and these districts gave their tone to all that was later to be called Modern Capitalism.

That system produced goods on a new and vaster scale, which made it possible for a much larger population to live. It concentrated the process of production, and therefore the unfortunate human agents now tied to the machine, within large towns which kept on growing and growing out of measure. It raised these vast accumulations of bricks and mortar, squalid architecture, drab streets and slums which set their mark upon all industrial society. Before the process was mature, industrial Capitalism, grown to such a new stature, had come to be identified in all men's minds with the group of social evils which are now bringing it to ruin. For this new machine age, spiritually mismanaged by Usury and Competition, subjected to no principles but greed, whether mercantile or banking, put mankind to a strain that was bound to become intolerable and to threaten all Society with catastrophe.

So far, so bad: but there was to come in, side by side with use of the new machinery, and indeed forming a special department of it, another factor which powerfully reinforced this main factor of mechanical production. The other factor was rapidity of communication both in goods and ideas.

The power of steam and the mechanical engines connected with it first made more secure, and on the average much more rapid, transport of goods and men by water. Such transport was no longer dependent upon the caprice of calm or adverse winds. It was subject, of course, to the caprice of exceptional stormy weather, but the average increase in rapidity and sureness through the use of steam made a new thing of water transport from the early years of the 19th century.

To this was soon added rapid transport by land also, born of the use of steam combined with the principle of the railway: a principle already used in the past to aid the running of trucks, before steam traction appeared. With the rapid transport of the steamship and the railroad Capitalism received another heavy and vastly increasing reinforcement. In an industrialized modern country, from a tenth to somewhat more, of the population was soon directly bound to the wage system of the great transport units. Further, the power of rapid transport in goods and in men made, obviously, for a concentration in control. One man and his subordinates will look after the business covering such and such an area, through its various branches. They are able to manage the business successfully, though with difficulty, even if that area be of such and such a size, and even if their travel over it has to be conducted through horse vehicles and by riding, and through the sailing ship. But with the coming of steam transport, the area over which one concentrated business could extend was indefinitely increased. An agent despatched from London to Manchester in the morning could act personally in Lancashire the same day and return to report in London that same night: before steam this double journey took three weeks.

As though this were not enough, there came in a new factor of rapidity in communication: electric communication, first in the shape of the electric telegraph* then, within living memory, in the shape of the telephone. These applications of science to commerce and industry yet further increased the hold of concentrated capital and of its central organ, finance, upon mankind. One speculative order which, in the old days, would have taken say a week to transmit and another week before the result could be received and acted upon, could pass after the introduction of the telegraph, over the whole continent. A man can attempt to make a corner in this or that commodity in all the markets of the world, though he remain sitting in one office in London or Chicago, during the few critical hours of his success or failure.

Over these last new instruments the small owner was quite powerless. He did not even compete with the large owner until he had, by luck or worse, made his own accumulation and forced his way competitively into a position where he could command the ear of those who distributed large credit. With the appearance of virtually instantaneous transport of ideas, of orders and information through no matter what distance, the last stone

---

* It was so called for years to distinguish it from its predecessor, the semaphore telegraph, which conveyed messages from one prominent height to another by signals. It was thus that the news of important naval action and orders were transmitted from the main English ports to the Admiralty in London during the revolutionary and Napoleonic wars.

had been added to the edifice of Industrial Capitalism and its superstructure of international finance and international exchange of goods.

The small owner appeared to be sunk forever. He remained precariously hanging on to the last structure of modern Capitalism as a parasite, and an anachronism at that. He struggled hard to maintain his human dignity and personal and family independence, in the family shop or the dying family craft, but he was hard put to it and disappeared in greater and greater numbers year by year. The end of the process was clear to all independent observers soon enough, and became at last obvious even to the mass of the oppressed themselves. That end could only be, apparently, the holding of all industrialized and urban mankind, such of it as was attached to our civilization, in the grasp of a few preëminent controllers of the means of production, distribution and exchange.

But even as this fatal turn to the long and degrading evil appeared thus before men as an unescapable doom, there was appearing, as there always does, the reaction of further development which proposed to undo all that had been done.

Industrial Capitalism itself, its system of morals, its negative greed, its whole being, had bred a child, fashioned in its own image, which child bid fair to murder his father. That child was the social philosophy first confusedly known as Socialism, later more completely and logically as Communism. To this vital issue of the whole affair we must next turn.

(b) COMMUNISM

The evils of the state of Society into which we have now fallen have been stated and examined. We have also stated and examined the process whereby those evils came upon us. They are the ultimate and mature fruits of that disruption of Christendom, three to four hundred years ago, through which our civilization progressively lost its religion and which is generally known as the Reformation.

Those evils are generally labelled under the title "Capitalism"; but before studying the proposed remedy for them we must make sure of our terms.

We mean by Capitalism a condition of Society under which the mass of free citizens, or at any rate a determining number of them, are not possessed of the means of production in any useful amount and therefore live upon wages doled out to them by the possessors of land and capital, men who thus exploit at a profit the dispossessed, known as the "Proletariat."

It is all-important to note that the word "Capitalism" thus used as the name for the great evil which, in its maturity, threatens the very existence of our society does *not* signify the rights of property. It signifies rather an abuse of property; property developed into an unnatural top-heavy form, under which it cannot normally function, and only threatens disaster. Capitalism no more means the affirmation of an individual, or a family's right to possess land, machinery, housing, clothing, reserves of food and the rest, than fatty degeneration of the heart means the normal function of the heart as the circulator of the blood in a healthy human body. Capitalism is an evil not because it defends the legal right to property, but because it is of its nature the use of that legal right for the defense of a privileged few against a much greater number who though free and equal citizens are without economic basis of their own. Therefore the root evil which we roughly term "Capitalism" should more accurately be termed "Proletarianism"; for the characteristic of the bad state of Society which we call today "Capitalist," is not the fact that the few own, but the fact that the many, though politically equal to their masters and free to exercise all the functions of a citizen, cannot enjoy full economic freedom.

It is the existence of so large a Proletariat as to give its tone to the whole Society, which makes that Society capitalist. It is not the natural and half-inevitable tendency of the Capitalist to exploit the situation which is the root of the evil; the root of the evil is the presence of vast numbers who are defenseless against exploitation.

Capitalism works for profit, and men have called this in their haste and confusion the main evil of the capitalist system. It is not so. There is nothing immoral or exasperating to human feelings in profit as a motive for production, distribution or exchange. The well-to-do shopkeeper travels by railway, the railway under the capitalist system makes a profit out of his journey—or ought to do so if it be properly conducted. The shareholder in a railway buys goods in the shopkeeper's shop; the shopkeeper makes a profit out of him. Both transactions are perfectly normal to human nature and the human conscience. The profit in the case of the railway is the legitimate reward attached to the saving of capital and the intelligent use of the same for human needs. The profit of the shopkeeper is the legitimate reward of similar activities in his line of business.

Or again, consider a situation which you may see in actual practice throughout many agricultural districts in the world: men using their own land, living in their own homes and producing some seasonal form of wealth, say livestock; and living as neighbours with other men of the same countryside who produce some other seasonal product, say wheat. There will for each of these independent owners, each of these economically free families, be a slack time in the year and a time of exceptional need for labor, a "peak" in the demand for labor, as it is called.

The livestock man, if he be a breeder of sheep, for instance, will need reinforcement of labor during lambing and shearing. If he be a breeder of cattle stalled in winter, he will need exceptional labor at haymaking time. The wheat-grower will need garnering of the grain. The man occupied in cereal farming will hire himself out at a wage to help the others during the haymaking season; Similarly the man occupied in livestock breeding will hire himself out during *his* slack seasons, when the beasts are all at pasture and the cereal harvest is being cut and garnered. Each party receives wages; out of each the wage-payer makes a profit; but there is no strain for there is mutual advantage.

Let us then repeat and firmly fix this main point: the evil, the root evil, of that to which the term *Capitalism* has come to be applied, is neither its functioning for profit nor its dependence upon legally protected private property; but the presence of a Proletariat, that is of men possessing political freedom, but dispossessed of economic freedom, and existing in such large numbers in any community as to determine the tone of all that community.

When the mass of men and families in a society think of themselves as wage-earners and are so regarded by the few who pay them their wages and make a profit out of them, that society is capitalist. It is capitalist not because a certain proportion possesses capital and uses it, but because the determining number* of the whole society is proletarian.

---

* The reader will recall my former use of this phrase, "determining number," but I will repeat it here as it is essential to the comprehension of the argument. A determining number in any matter, economic, social, religious or what not, is a number such that it gives its tone to Society in general. It does not mean a majority; it does not mean any fixed proportion; it is discoverable only by experience, inspection and familiarity with the activity in question. For instance, the number of married adults in a society may not come to half the total of that society, which might count in children, bachelors, spinsters, widows, widowers, etc., making

Now let us consider the evils afflicting such a society and appreciate them in their due proportion.

Here as in everything human the spiritual outweighs the material. It is the spiritual evils attaching to proletarianism which are the chief cause of its increasing instability, and of these spiritual evils two are particularly prominent; (1) the sense of injustice aroused in men politically free, but deprived of economic freedom; (2) the indignant protest of the man who knows himself to be a full citizen and is yet exploited by another more fortunate than himself, who has no claim save his superior wealth to exercise such power. There is a lack of moral sanction which renders the situation intolerable. When Status is generally recognized, a moral sanction for the relations between superior and inferior, even if these be economic evils, can be discovered; the duty of the feudal superior, the loyalty of the feudal inferior, are moral realities, familiar to both parties and believed by both parties to be the guarantees of their civilized life. There is no such bond when Contract has taken the place of Status, and when one man works for the profit of another merely because he has had no choice but to contract so to do.

Another main spiritual evil attaching to a proletarian state, that is, to "Capitalism," is the increasing contrast between luxury and superfluity on the part of those in economic power, and the indigence or mere subsistence of those economically dependent upon them. Here again,

---

a majority—but the institution of marriage none the less gives its tone to that society.

The proportion of lawless men, outrage, etc., in a particular district may apply only to a minority and even to a comparatively small minority; and yet that proportion may be so considerable as to create a "determining number," so that the society is properly called "a lawless one." A good example of this is the banditry which was with such difficulty extirpated in Corsica. The number of bandits were never more than a few score at the most, in a population of many thousands, yet they were sufficient to make everyone talk (and rightly talk) of that country as "infested with bandits."

were it not for civic equality between the two parties, the contrast would not involve so great a strain. But if civic equality be proclaimed and accepted by both parties, especially by the less fortunate of the two, then a very strong sense of injustice is aroused. The man who works in all weathers at a wage, transporting his wealthy fellow-citizens to their places of amusement or worse, has this contrast actively before his eyes continually, and the mass of a proletarian population in any great urban industrial center is conscious of the contrast in varying degrees.

Moreover (as I have said) this contrast is increasing, and the lack of moral sanction to it, is all the more glaring because there is less and less correspondence between the enjoyment of superfluity and the talent or industry which might be put forward as an excuse for the advantages enjoyed.

A lucky speculation brought off without a stroke of genuine work and having no productive value to mankind will create a millionaire. The chance of locality in a rapidly developing country will do the same thing. What is worse, the reprehensible activities which permit vast and rapid accumulations are in great and increasing proportion, for they include not only the speculative element, (not in itself immoral), but the exercise of cunning and a large measure of fraud by widespread propaganda and downright sharp-practice: what is called "keeping on the right side of the law"—and not only always that. To these main spiritual evils attaching to the system as we see it before us today in its maturity, may be added yet another spiritual evil, somewhat less, but weighty all the same. It is the instability of the affair. Great economic power over other men appears suddenly in such and such hands—to disappear almost as suddenly.

Another spiritual evil not to be neglected is the impersonal character running through the whole: the divorce of human personality from production, the lack of a human bond between those who labor and those who profit by their labor; the anonymity of the great corporations under which the wage-earner works, or the remoteness of the individual (when it is an individual) who commands, from those who are commanded.

On another and lower plane, but essential to an understanding of the situation, are the material evils of the system. It involves inevitable recurring destitution for many and the permanent peril of destitution even for those who are not for the moment suffering it. Such destitution may be met by relief, but it is in the nature of the situation that the relief must be insufficient for decent living, i.e., for the standard properly attached to civic life in a community of free men. Since it is to the advantage of the wage-payer to pay as little as possible, even well paid labor will have no more than what is regarded in a particular society as the reasonable level of subsistence. The lower ranks of labor will commonly have less, and if public relief were afforded even up to the wage-level of the lowest ranks of labor, that relief would compete in the labor market; check or dry up the supply of wage-labor. It would tend to render the performance of work by the wage-earner redundant; for if relief were on a scale approaching regular wages the average man would not do work for a sum which he could obtain without working.

Such are the main evils attaching to an economic system based upon proletarian labor. There is a whole department of other evils on which we have no space here to digress, though they are socially of high importance; there is the standardization of life, the increasing lack of choice and diversity in articles produced, the mechanical spirit unnaturally imposed upon the non-mechanical, organic, nature of man, and so on. But we will confine ourselves to the main evils here noted because they most clearly explain the strain which has been set up and which cannot be resolved in one way or another. For every strain is necessarily and inevitably resolved either at the expense of good readjustment or bad readjustment—which last we call catastrophe.

Now the resolving of the strains set up by Capitalism may be effected in one of three ways. The strains are due to the juxtaposition of two incompatible elements, political freedom and economic lack of freedom: the political freedom of the proletarian, which enables him to contract and binds him to the contract he makes, coupled with the fact that the proletarian is deprived of the means of livelihood and must live at the will of another. The strain can only be resolved by the elimination of one of these two incompatible factors; either we must restore property to the bulk of the families in the state which are now proletarian, or we must suppress freedom.

If we are to suppress freedom, there are two ways in which we may do it; we may either suppress political freedom (that is the right to contract and the obligation to fulfil contracted engagements) by depriving the proletariat of this right and leaving only the Capitalist a fully free citizen; or we may hand over the means of production, distribution and exchange to the community— that is, hand it over to public officers and suppress freedom in all, Capitalist and proletarian alike, thus reducing everyone to a common proletarian condition, dependent no longer upon many capitalist controllers, but only upon one omnipotent single capitalist master—the State.

But if we are to retain freedom, then we can only do so by keeping the determining mass of the citizens the possessors of property with personal control over it, as individuals or as families. For property is the necessary condition of economic freedom in the full sense of that term. He that has not property is under economic servitude to him who has property, whether the possessor of it be another individual or the State.

There are thus, as I have said, three methods by which the strain may be relieved; one which consists in the reintroduction of private property on a large scale where it has been lost, and the ending of the proletariat by thus turning its members into owners; and two others, the suppression of freedom in the masses for the benefit of the few, or the suppression of freedom in all under the domination of one common master.

The latter proposition is known today as "Communism." And let it not be objected that this solution, Communism, is no necessary third issue because property might be held collectively in small amounts, or at any rate in units less than that of universal social control. It could not be so; for either the spirit at work is a spirit of economic unification throughout the State, whereby the private choice and activity of the family is eliminated, or the spirit at work is one protecting and encouraging the independence of the family. If the second spirit be at work, some measure of inequality cannot but arise: a multiple diversity, in the case of a large state, an indefinitely large diversity, of private interests and methods. You may incorporate the craftsmen of one activity, say builders, in one guild, or in a collection of smaller guilds. You may charter the guilds in a Communist State so that each be called self-governing. But even so, either their moral life would repose upon the conception of economic independence in their units, or, on the control of those units by the guild. And if the second solution be adopted it is inevitable that the regulation of the various activities of the various crafts and occupations shall fall under the general control of the society as a whole. For either the balance must be preserved by the perpetual interplay of very numerous diverse particular forces, or it must be imposed by the sovereignty of one.

The two ideas are not supplementary, they are hostile. The one is the ideal of a disciplined body such as is an army; but an army not as actual armies are, (separate from general Society and exceptional in structure to the world around it), rather of an army, the private soldiers and officers of which cover the whole area of Society. The other presupposes a perpetual flux and interplay between the various units, which units are the families composing the State.

Rules may indeed be made to safeguard the latter—the system of Property—so that as large a number as possible of those units remain proprietors; competition may be restrained in the degree necessary to prevent the eating up of the small man by the great; but on one of two opposed, contradictory, and mutually destructive moral attitudes must Society repose: either the attitude which regards the citizen as having for the end of his being the good of the State, and the State as master of the citizen; or the other opposite ideal of the State composed of free citizens. Either the State admitting exceptions to its complete economic domination, or free owners reluctantly admitting necessary exceptions to their freedom and permitting some measure of control by the State.

It is a fundamental error in the appreciation of mankind to conceive of any political doctrine, and the denial of it, as a reconcilable modification of the doctrine and the denial. There are two spirits facing each other, and those two spirits are opposed.

Of the two solutions, which must be obvious to every observer of the modern industrial quarrel, that of Communism follows the line of least resistance.

The restoration of property would be a complicated,

arduous and presumably a lengthy business; the transformation of a Capitalist Society into a Communist one
needs nothing but the extension of existing conditions.

Here you already have a proletariat, used to organization under the discipline of those who control the means of
production; you have but to substitute the various titles
to possession held by those who now control, for one
title of possession vested in the State and your end is
accomplished. Life goes on exactly as it went on before
for the mass of men, because the mass of men in an
industrialized Capitalist Society live in a dependence and
semi-servitude already, hardly distinguishable from the
full servitude which Communism would involve. The Communist State would have no motive to reduce further the
leisure or the amenities of life, such as they are, of the
existing proletariat; on the contrary, save out of malice
or hostility to individuals who disapproved of it, Communism would presumably in general ameliorate the lot
of the wage-earner, and would (as its predicators take
for granted) maintain the full activity of the system under
collective ownership, which we now discover under divided
and private ownership by the few. A group of great
capitalist railway companies can become a State group of
railways by a stroke of the pen; the thing is done in a
moment, whether by immediate confiscation or by gradual
buying out of the existing shareholders. The thing has
recently been done before our eyes in Belgium, for
example, where the railways passed easily by purchase
from private shareholders to the State. One has but to
extend the field until it shall cover the whole of Society.
The more perfected the capitalist system becomes, the
wider its area of activity, the less does the old argument
in favor of private enterprise apply; the more exactly
similar does the new Communist State appear to the
Capitalist State of which it seems to be the natural des-

cendant, and of which it takes over all the morals except the relics of private property.

As to the consolidation of so simple a change, from Capitalism to Communism, that is effected by a fundamental law, brief and easy of comprehension by all. Abolish the right of inheritance, and Communism will have come to stay.

Such is the abstract or arithmetical position, the mere pattern, on which the Communist idea of a new state reposes.

Those who accept it as an ideal might, it would seem, propose nothing but good; they eliminate at a stroke the injustices, the embitterments, the indignations attaching to Capitalism; they relieve the human conscience of those evils; they restore peace.

It has recently been said by a prominent protagonist of Communism in Western Europe: "Today, with us, every shopkeeper is the enemy of every other shopkeeper; every employed man the enemy of every employer; under Communism no man is the enemy of another."

Put thus, the case for Communism appears overwhelmingly strong; yet we know, as a mere historical fact, the advance of the Communist idea has been very slow and has met with the toughest resistance from the conscience of what was once Christendom; we know that it is rejected with the highest determination, we know that it cannot be imposed without violence pushed to extreme limits; we know by experience that the way to it lies through wholesale massacre.

How are we to reconcile these contradictions?

By understanding that when we say the word "Communism" we of necessity mean much more than—indefinitely more than—a mere pattern, a mere abstract arrangement; we connote something which has been in the eyes of humanity, which necessarily is to the Christian tradition, to the normal man hearing of it today, inhuman. In point of fact Communism in this concrete sense cannot be established, nor ever has been, save by murderous violence applied under pure despotism. The effort to establish it will, among men still possessing the traditions of our culture, that is, the inheritance of Christendom, be resisted to the death; and to understand why that should be so, let us consider not the mere word Communism, the mere conception of common ownership (which is as old as the world and has as little content as a vacuum) but the actual thing, the innumerable connotations in living reality, which the practice of Communism involves.

To make this appreciation we must begin by recapitulating the historical development of the whole business, that is the establishment of Capitalism and the corresponding growth of Communism as a remedy for the evils of Capitalism.

The reader is acquainted with the first of these processes; it is indeed the matter of all the last few sections of this book. The unity of Western Christendom was wrecked by the explosion which we call the Reformation. Slowly, as the dust subsided and we were able to survey the ruins, we could perceive certain consequences emerging. There being no longer any common moral authority nor a common moral tradition sufficiently vigorous to restrain the coming evils, they grow apace and the first of them was the creation of a Proletariat; not (as we were at pains to point out) that there was no Proletariat in the older and better state of affairs; for such a class, men of the same political standing as their fellows, but, unlike their fellows, deprived of property and therefore of security in livelihood, had come into existence before the end of the Middle Ages in a few commercial centers. Before the Reformation, the Proletariat was highly restricted in numbers and confined to few places. Had it expanded under the old conditions it would have been taken in hand and securely established within the general rules of Christian society by new guilds. When that society, however, broke up, there was nothing left to restrain the growth of the Proletariat wherever favorable conditions could be found for that growth. There were indeed many districts, mainly agricultural in character, where the loss of the old morals with their social safeguards, the guild and the rest of it, did not produce a Proletariat; such was the case with the Alpine valleys, with most of the population of Scandinavia and many other areas. But wherever life was complicated and economic forces active, a Proletariat took root and expanded under Protestantism until it became the dominant feature in the social landscape. This was particularly the case with England, which as it was the only Roman (and therefore anciently civilized) province to abandon the common unity of Western Christendom, could bring to the new non-Catholic developments an energy far superior to that of the outer, non-Roman, more barbaric lands.

In England therefore, based on the vast economic Revolution of the 16th century by the sudden enrichment of a new class which battened on the spoil of all collegiate property—hospitals, and schools as well as monastic establishments and religious endowment of all kinds—a Proletariat was formed even *upon the land.*

Never let it be forgotten that this agricultural proletariat was the source, model and breeding ground of the urban proletariat that was to follow. The thing happened in the 17th century; it was a product of the second and third generation after the loss of their ancestral faith by the English. England was fundamentally Catholic in ethic during the first years of Elizabeth: 1560 to 1570. A lifetime later, in the first third of the 17th century a large but enthusiastic minority of anti-Catholics had arisen, and, what was more important still, that minority held all the reins of social life, from the central government down to the smallest village school. The mass of people were more or less indifferent. There remained on the other wing a very large minority who would have been pleased with the return of the old religion but who were no longer particularly conscious of the principle of European unity. They were indeed so strongly filled with the local patriotism of the day that they suffered from a spiritual struggle between their English patriotism and their international religious leanings. This was the England in which the Civil Wars were fought; great numbers of sympathizers with the old religion were killed off, and vastly more ruined. With the latter part of the 17th century England as a nation had lost her old economic and ethical philosophy which was to produce the modern industrial world.

Under the effect of that new philosophy the remaining large mass of economically free peasants disappeared. There were perhaps by the year 1700 not a quarter of the agricultural population possessed of the land they tilled, and the proportion was rapidly diminishing, for the remainder were living at a wage.

Then came the full growth of the new forces which were to support social change, and at the same time to extend the numbers of the proletariat and establish still further their dependence upon a small class of owners. Overseas commerce and banking we saw to be the chief of these new adjuncts to the new system. The fortunes built up by the one and the financial control of the other made the coexistence of a very large proletarian body and their capitalist masters certain and secure. On top of this came the new use of machinery, then rapidity of communications.

So much for the material development, which had all

proceeded in due line from the spiritual change of preceding generations. But there went on at the same time another development following also in direct line from that spiritual change; this other development it was which gave its moral atmosphere to the new system, not only in England, but in all Western Europe.

The break-up of unity had rendered men bewildered, confused and therefore at least doubtful, if not in the matter of doctrine at any rate on the principle of certitude therein. The quality of Faith was lost, or rather faded. It grew less and less operative as time went on, even in those parts of European society which kept to the traditional practise of religion. With that loss went the loss of the social guarantees which the old religion had bred. Usury and excessive universal competition, for instance, came to be taken for granted throughout our society. Under those conditions it was presumable that small property would decay and wage-slavery take its place whenever the conditions were favorable.

The breakdown of religion having created a Proletariat on the one side, permitted on the other side a social arrangement whereby those who possessed capital in sufficient amounts and who controlled the reserves of livelihood would as a matter of course exploit those who did not. Status having been dissolved and replaced by Contract, the old human bonds having been replaced by mechanical arrangements, what we call Capitalism followed as a matter of course, built up by the proletarian conditions which had come first and which, with Capitalism were an ultimate product of the weakening or disappearance of that religion which had been the foundation, the bond and creator of our ancient culture.

"All Wars," it was said to me in boyhood by a great man, old and very wise (Cardinal Manning), "are ultimately religious." So it certainly was in this case. The enormous evils of a rising Capitalism proceeded from the disruption followed by the loss of religion, and war threatens from that cause.

It was in the same atmosphere that there arose the proposed remedy, even worse than the disease. Capitalism had arisen through the misuse and exaggeration of certain rights, notably the right of property—the basis of economic freedom—and the right of contract, which is one of the main functions of economic freedom. Therefore, even under Capitalism, so long as the old principles were remembered it was possible to recall the principles whereby Society had once been sane and well ordered. But as a Godless greed pursued its career from excess to excess, it provoked a sort of twin hostile brother, equally Godless, born in the same atmosphere of utter disregard for the foundational virtues of humility and charity. This hostile twin brother of Capitalism was destined to be called Communism, and is today setting out to murder its elder.

I have said that Communism, the thing, the concrete institution (for it is no less) which has arisen among us today, is of necessity vastly more than a mere abstract proposition of mere community in the means of production; it is an intense, creative, applicable creed with a defined and vivid philosophy, such that those who adopt it are necessarily the enemies of the Christian religion and particularly of that which is the source and principle of being within the Christian tradition—the Catholic Church.

What today we call Communism does not only deny the liberties of man, it denies the dignity of man. Its whole career, not from its inception, but from the moment when its full nature became manifest, stands witness to this truth; Communist society on the model of those already in existence (as in Russia) and those struggling to come into existence (as in Spain at the moment) is primarily, before it is anything else, the enemy of God and His Christ.

In this there is no ambiguity left any longer; there is no doubt. The forces are set out in line of battle; the preliminary dispersed skirmishes are over; the distinction is clean drawn.

Communism is proposed as the universal, obvious and final remedy for the mortal evils of Capitalism; but that remedy, as the great Encyclical so admirably puts it, "is even worse than disease," because in the very heart of things it opposes the Creator of things, and in proposing an immediate good, sets out to kill the fundamental source of happiness in mankind. Heretical dispute and distortion of certain Catholic Doctrines produced Capitalism and a consequent indifference to those Doctrines confirmed it; but a complete denial of *all* Catholic Doctrine and an intense Atheism produced Materialist Communism, now proposed as a remedy.

The war upon which we are already engaged and which will soon absorb the attentions of us all is a religious war. Of this indeed most of the potential combatants are not yet aware, but it is only a matter of time for all to be aware of it and openly proclaim their adhesion to the one side or the other: nay, enroll themselves upon one side or the other. We perceive this inner central character running through Communism during the whole of its rapid progress.

At the beginning came partial and sporadic protest against the evils which Industrial Capitalism has launched. Those protests have no cohesion, they crop up in the shape of various theories from writers who are not themselves engaged in industrial processes, writers who are neither

capitalist nor wage-earners, sometimes middle class poli-
ticians vaguely groping for impossible remedies or spinning phrases too vague to have any true application. You
have the French extravagants with their petty followings;
you have the experiments (and failures) of the English,
such as the movement of Robert Owen; you have in the
much larger merely political movements, such as the
Chartist movement, a certain distant admixture of economic revolt. But the thing does not take on shape and
body until the mid-19th century; and when it does so, it
still calls itself by an ambiguous name; the term "Socialism" becomes a common label for the various theories of
attack upon the principle of property, the various policies
of communal control at the expense of the family and
individual freedom.

The general air of the time over the whole of Society
far beyond the boundaries of mere economic effort favors
such an advance against human dignity and sane social
life, notably against the family. The permanence of marriage was questioned, the education of children was taken
out of the hands of their parents who were put back to a
lower and lower position in the moulding of the lives of the
young. In the particular economic field the rights of
property were no longer founded upon the nature and
dignity of man, the safeguarding of his freedom of will,
his personality, but upon arguments concerning the community alone. That is a false basis, and it has bred the
evil fruit which all false philosophy breeds. That philosophy even appeared in the monstrous form of asserting
that the indefinite extension of private greed would work
out to the advantage of all. Such was the very central
principle of what was known in England as "The Manchester School." It wrought havoc not only in the social
relations of men, but even in his external surroundings;

the repulsive industrial towns of the North of England are a monument to the ill that can be done by false doctrine.

Against the increasing and soon to be intolerable evils of Capitalism, the nebulous congeries of Reforms to which was given the common name of "Socialist," were manifestly insufficient. But men hesitated to push the proposed change to its full conclusion. The reformers of the 19th century used vaguely such formulæ as "from each according to his capacities; to each according to his needs." They promised a society in which there should still be as much private ownership as would satisfy the equally vague instincts of their hearers, and attempted in some way to combine the principle of property with the implications of its opposite. They preached antagonism without conflict and wandered at large amid a host of similar self-contradictions.

This vague Socialism could not last. That which was to thrust it disdainfully aside was already born and growing rapidly to maturity. That which was to destroy Socialism was the specifically announced assumption—let us call it the Dogma—which comes forward in double shape just after the middle of the century; the full doctrine of Materialism.

It commonly takes a lifetime for some innovation among men to grow to full stature. The older spirits trained in other thoughts must die out and a new generation not only grow up, but become mature and have time to find itself and even to become at last the revered seniors who are listened to with authority, before a novel doctrine, good or bad, can be fully established.

That is what happened with Materialism; it has become the leading philosophy of the Western World, whether acknowledged or not. It has produced its own cosmogony, its own interpretation of the origin and nature of man, and therefore its own economic and social scheme.

As to its cosmogony—and that is, its explanation of the origin and nature of man and of the world in which he lives—we may take the central and pivoting date to be the appearance of Darwin's book, "On the Origin of Species"; as to the particular social and economic scheme which went parallel with this, we may take the contemporary publication of the book "Capital," by Karl Marx.

Let it first of all be emphasized that neither of these writers is of the first class. They were neither of them illuminating or creative thinkers; they were neither of them original; they were both of them inordinately lengthy, prosy and dull. They and their books are not to be cited here as causes; they were nothing half so respectable; but they *were* symptoms. That they should have had so great a vogue and that so many effects should be traced to them is a proof of how consonant they were to the ambient spirit of their time.

It was just seventy-five years ago that the business began; the full fruits of it we are enjoying today.

Charles Darwin was a man who had been steeped through family inheritance in the conceptions for the proof of which he gathered great masses of evidence, falsely applied. He set out to combine two quite different propositions: first that there existed ample evidence of transformation from one physical shape to another in animate nature, so that the most different forms *might* proceed from a common ancestor; secondly, that this differentation of form proceded by a very slow process of minute changes, the cumulative effect of which could only be discovered after immense spaces of time, because each step is the consequence of a blind, purely mechanical process, wherein no perceptible action of the will, whether of creator or created could be discovered. Hence the title of his book, which is not "The Origin of Species," but "The Origin of Species by Natural Selection."

The first of these hypotheses, called "Transformism," though unproven, is possible or probable. The second, called "Natural Selection," which is the core of the whole argument, is demonstrably false.

The essential of Darwin's great haystack of a book, with its innumerable researches into examples of similarity of structure suggesting common origins, is *not* "evolution" —a word which simply means growth and may be used to mean anything or nothing. No; the essential of it is the doctrine that living organisms change by the effect of survival among those best fitted for some new condition, and the dying off of the rest.

Some tiny proportion in a particular group of birds displays some tiny beginnings of webbing between the claws; as the climate grew damper this gave a survival advantage to the lucky possessors of this exceptional formation, and their progeny enjoy increased advantages, while those who were not so formed have less chance of surviving. So, at long last—at very long last—a new kind of bird would appear with fully webbed feet.

This was the essential of a theory insisted upon with the utmost industry and repetition, that *neither the instinct of the animal, still less any plan or will behind the universe, effected the change; the whole thing was mechanical and innocent of design.*

The book being typical of the spirit of the time, had, of course, an immediate popular success; and the theory being disastrously simple, appealed to all. It had the merit of eliminating all necessity for a Creator, and therefore for responsibility to Him.

In vain were the counter-arguments, which are sufficient on a brief examination to explode Darwin's unproved affirmation, put forward, from Quatrefages onwards. That all-powerful force called Fashion had set in and even plain arithmetic was not listened to.* Neither was the argument from fossils. It ought to have been self-evident that if this theory were true there would be before our eyes today an infinitely large number of intermediate forms. Those who defended the theory said that we did not experience such forms because the process was extremely slow; when they were told that in that case fossils would give evidence of an infinitely large number of intermediate forms, a perpetual flux from shape to shape, they answered by saying that fossils would show this when we had enough of them. By this time we have more than enough and we know that such a flux has never been, for evidence of it is absent; we know that from the earliest ages the fixed form (often producing other fixed forms) is the rule, and very slow change by Natural Selection is left without any evidence to bring into court.

But, I repeat, Fashion is during its brief reign omnipotent; Darwin was taken for a great man—which, whatever else he was, he certainly was not—and he was put forward as having proved what he did not prove. But what he had done was to supply ammunition for the triumphant materialist advance, which became omnipresent in the field of biology and all that is allied to biology, including the origin and nature of man.

Contemporaneously with Darwin appeared the work of Karl Marx. Here again you get a man who is essentially derivative, with nothing creative or original about him; a

---

* A digression on the arithmetical argument alone would be too long to set down here; briefly it can be put thus: The exceptional product of two exceptionally endowed parents—such as a cock and a hen who glory in slightly webbed feet—diminishes in *geometrical* proportion with every generation. If one in a hundred display this tiny original advantage, in the next generation only one in ten thousand will fully show the benefit, let alone increase it; and in the third generation only one in a million.

hanger-on of the French revolutionary thinkers and particularly of that half-French, half-Scottish man, Louis Blanc,
and an heir to Prudhon, of the famous *"La proprieté,
c'est le vol."* The family name of Marx was Mordecai,
"Marx" being one of those false names, which whether
from fear of persecution or a dramatic sense, Jews so often
adopt. In this case it was adopted by his family rather
than by himself. He set out to prove with a great mass
of examples, just as Darwin did in his particular department, the bad history that social transformation was due
to blind mechanical causes, rather than the will of man;
that evil effects proceeded from material environment
and not from false doctrine or an evil disposition of the
mind. Hence the twin book to "The Evolution of Species,"
"Das Kapital," a Jewish book written in German with the
immense industry, tenacity and sincerity characteristic of
his blood, produced for the most part in the British
museum, for in England Marx lived as an exile from his
native Germany. His work was too long for his life; it
was completed by his friend and admirer Engels, and
being cosmopolitan in authorship and appeal, was soon
translated into all languages. What Darwin had supplied
to Materialism in biology, Marx supplied to it in sociology;
and the two combined not to form as causes, but to present
as symptoms the common Materialism which in the later
19th century was to sweep over the cultivated mind of
Europe.

In the particular case of social revolution the effect of
this materialist triumph was to level all obstacles to the
advance of Communism. Communism was the logical
full development of the halting clouded and variagated
stuff which had been current under the name of Socialism.
All that had prevented the suppressed Proletariat (or
rather their *non-Proletarian* conscious leaders) from going
"the whole hog," had been the remaining strength of

Christendom and the Christian ethic: to put it simply, the command "Thou shalt not steal"; the remaining strength of what is native to the Western European man, a respect for property as the guarantee of human dignity and freedom. But with the absence of a Divine basis for them, the moral sanctions failed; and in the absence of a moral sanction for property, property could not stand. Tradition still kept it precariously erect, though ill defended by false theories as materialist as were their opponents. Then came the shock of the Great War.

It is a character proper to all shocks that they tend to precipitate whatever had been in solution, to realize in catastrophic fashion whatever had been latent, to relieve what had hitherto been only urgent and increasing strains. A shock on so huge a scale as the Great War did this work instantly and thoroughly; the Proletariat was not only shaken into consciousness of its sufferings and chances of release, but had its sense of opposition multiplied a hundredfold by the agonies of the prolonged conflict.

Already more than half a lifetime earlier a similar shock on a minor scale had produced the Commune in Paris; the outrages and cruel repression of that uprising, the murder of priests as representing the old morality, the burning down of public monuments, etc. Now, after the Great War, the same thing appeared on a much greater scale in the Russian Revolution. That revolution was led by a small international clique, largely Jewish in composition, and energized almost wholly by its Jewish members; for in these were found not only an intense motive for revenge against the old regime, but also cosmopolitan experience, instruments of secret action and that combination of tenacity, lucidity and strong instincts for social justice which have made the Jews so formidable a revolutionary force in one crisis after another in the West.

At first sight the traveller might have said that Russia

was the worst of all fields in which to begin the experiment of atheist and materialist Communism. Its vast population, in which the Christians alone were over a hundred million, were attached to their ancestral religion of the Greek or Orthodox type; they were peasant, and therefore affected by the evils of modern industrialism less than many populations of Europe—if indeed they can be called European. It would seem to be most unpromising material for what followed; for what followed was the establishment of a Communist regime with all its characteristics pushed to an extreme; beginning with wholesale massacres on a scale hitherto unknown among Christian men, comparable only to the Asiatic orgies of the Mongol invaders seven centuries ago.

After this wild riot of universal butchery came a complete scheme for fully despotic control over the human wills subject to them by a tiny group of energetic and determined men, who have since been known as "The Soviet Government." All private property ceased at a blow, in theory at least and in law. Its resurrection was rendered impossible by the refusal of the State to guarantee inheritance. But it is an utterly false picture which presents the tremendous event as mainly social and economic; it was in the mind and action of its leaders primarily religious. Their business was to destroy the Christian name and the spirit of Christ in Society. Even the teaching of His religion to little children was universally put down by force. The atheism which was the driving power of all this was not secret or subsidiary, it was openly proclaimed and enthroned in the very heart of the affair.

An effort was made to spread this new materialist atheism with its Communist consequence "by the sword" (as the metaphor goes), that is, by the invasion of neighboring countries with consequent further massacres and the extension of the area of despotic Soviet control. The process has been excellently compared to the sudden explosion of Mahommedanism in the early seventh century. This armed attempt at expansion was checked by Catholic Poland, the most immediately exposed victim, in what has been well called "one of the decisive battles of the world."* The Soviet armies were crushingly defeated just as they were upon the point of seizing the Polish capital.

As everyone knows, a second flare-up of militant Communism took place in Spain during the months wherein the present book is being written, and the series of lectures upon which it is based delivered.

In the Spanish field there appeared exactly the same symptoms as had appeared in Russia; massacre, arson, despotic control and the rest of it. But there was this difference, that in Spain the various forces which for very different reasons supported the national tradition and the religion thereof took the initiative before things had gone very far. A revolt by a group of officers in the army followed by a large proportion of their men (but also abandoned by a large minority) suddenly struck hard at the master of the new revolution. They used all means to hand, including the Mahommedan troops in Africa, and were as ruthless in their counter-action as the revolutionaries had been in theirs, proclaiming their determination to stamp out "the bestial Marxian thing."

The issue is not yet decided. Perhaps before these words appear in print it may be, so far as Spain is concerned, decided definitely in one way or the other: but even if it be decided there, it most certainly will not be universally decided, from action in that one Spanish field alone.

A universal battle has to be fought out and as it proceeds will be, like all universal battles, based upon universal philosophies. It will therefore be confused in many of its

---

* The phrase is that of the English politician and financier d'Abernon, Ambassador at Berlin when the battle was fought.

issues. There will be strange alliances and counter-alliances, mixed motives of every moral value from the basest to the highest, and individuals *on either side* following noble aspirations, tangled instincts, and the basest and most abominable of temptations—from the satisfaction of mere hatred to the Satanic delight in cruelty. But while it will be thus muddled and confused, as (I repeat) all universal struggles must be, there will appear in it none the less, more and more clearly as the years proceed, the division between the two spirits, utterly and essentially enemy the one to the other, each working for the total extinction of the other: Christ and anti-Christ.

In the Cathedral of Cefalu on the north coast of Sicily, which was built under the first Norman Kings in the early crusading time, there is placed over the half-dome of the apse a great mosaic representing Christ in Judgment.

Under it, along the border, runs, in mosaic also, a motto made up of a Latin hexameter and pentameter. It is, of course, anonymous; I have never discovered its authorship. It runs as follows:

Factus Homo, Factor Hominis, Factique Redemptor,
Corporeus judico, corpora corda Deus.

"*Having been made Man, I, the Maker of Man, and the Redeemer of what I made, judge, having myself a body, the bodies and souls of men: for I am God.*"

It is the complete doctrine of the Incarnation.

Now the Incarnation raises humanity to its highest conceivable level and is at the same time the central doctrine of the Catholic Church. They that would malform, distort, and torture humanity into a mechanical mould, grinding its very soul, are necessarily at war with the Incarnation. Herein you may discover the implacable hostility between Communism and the Faith: for it is the function and glory of the Faith to consecrate and therefore to defend the nature of man.

So much for the immediate, intensely nourished, and now rapidly rising proposed remedy for the intolerable evils of Capitalism: the Communist remedy.

But there is an alternative. That alternative is the remedy of returning to Christian things.

V

RESTORATION

WE HAVE SEEN how, by a long chain of cause and effect, Christendom (if it may still be so called) has arrived at a crisis in which it may founder: that is, in which the civilization which we associate with all our past and by which we live may collapse under the attempted false remedy of Communism. This false remedy is for the moment the most obvious; it is the remedy that appeals immediately, not only to those who suffer from the injustices and intolerable strain of Capitalism, but to those generous minds in whom injustice to others is a sufficient motive for action. Obviously Communism also appeals as a remedy to the international revolutionary who first conceived it and who is directing it.

These three forces combined constitute a very formidable power driving the modern Capitalist state, in its difficulties and approaching collapse, towards Communism. The solution having behind it the honest enthusiasm of those who protest against injustice, receives from that source the one invaluable moral ingredient essential to the success of any movement: spiritual enthusiasm. For that increasing number of minds which incline to the Communist experiment, not through any needs of their own, but in protest against manifest evils, have a powerful source of inspiration. They are inspired by the desire to right a wrong; and a driving force of that sort, however mistaken the policy which it adopts, is creative and inhabited by a concrete spirit.

Then the second element (which is much the more apparent in the movement), the proletarian rebellion against the inhuman conditions of Capitalism, provides the second factor, numbers. Wherever modern industrial society has spread, wherever there is a large transport organization or a large organization for mechanical production or a large financial organization, there you have the overwhelming majority determined upon the drastic amendment of the conditions under which they live. The easiest, most apparent, and most direct path to such amendment is Communism.

Lastly, you have the directors of the movement, cosmopolitan, conscious of a clear philosophical position which is materialist and atheist; these furnish the staffwork without which no aggressive effort, military or civilian, can be made. These give the plans and issue the orders which are obeyed not only by those who consciously accept them as orders, but by a much greater number who follow them by suggestion.

Against so formidable a combination rising in power every day what are those who perceive the peril it involves to do? What alternative shall they propose? Manifestly, it would be impossible to achieve anything without some plan, without the scheme of new institutions. To tell the sufferer to be patient does not cure his disease. To continue on the old lines of the social structure, which has broken down in morals and in practice, is to invite disaster. What are the new institutions, the new conceptions, guiding those institutions and creating them, which the reformer who perceives that Communism is death may advance as a sufficient remedy for the sickness of the modern world?

They fall into three main groups, and all these three are connected at their root by one Catholic philosophy, which salutary reform must adopt, and without which the remedies proposed will fail.

The three main groups of reform are: First, the better distribution of property; secondly, the public control of monopolies; thirdly, the reëstablishment of those principles and that organization which underlay the conception of a guild.

If we have those three things actively at work—well distributed property, strong government controlling the despotism of monopoly, and coöperative work under the form of the guild—our end will have been achieved. On that triple foundation we can erect a new system that shall be strong and permanent because it will be just and because it will be consonant to the nature of man. We shall have built a state in which men can live in as much normal happiness as is to be expected of man's fallen nature and of the temporal conditions by which he is constrained in this life. We shall have no paradise, for paradise is not to be reëntered in this world. We shall not have done with the chief moral evils of mankind, for these come not from material conditions or political arrangements, but from the corruption of the heart. What we shall have done, however, is to get rid of that unbearable feeling of social injustice, protest against which threatens to wreck us altogether.

Here most men would halt, saying: "Well, if those three groups of remedies combined are sufficient, let us set about to apply them. Let us form the rules and even elaborate the details of institutions which will provide, and laws which will foster, well divided property, the control of monopoly and the guild. Then our work will be done, our task achieved."

Such a conclusion is an error, and an error which persisted in will prove fatal, because institutions neither arise of themselves nor are preserved by mere verbal regulations. Institutions rise from a certain spirit inhabiting Society, a spirit of which they are the product; and they are maintained by men's acceptance of that spirit and their formation at the hands of that spirit.

In our best time, when there was indeed a good division of property, control of monopoly, and a flourishing of the guild, all the framework of that society grew from a certain philosophy held strongly as a religion. It was the philosophy, the religion of the Catholic Church.

Therefore does it remain true that we shall only recover a moral society, secure small property, the control of monopoly, and the guild if we also recover the general spirit of Catholicism. In other words, you will not remedy the world until you have converted the world.

It would seem, therefore, that the conclusion of this study must be: First, an examination in their order of each of the three main elements in the reform—the restoration of property, the control of monopoly, the reëstablishment of the guild; but after these a coördination of all three within the framework of Catholic thought, whence indeed they proceed and without which they can neither be planted nor live.

In other words, we have to end this study by appreciating how the small owner may be brought into being and survive, how his grand enemy that threatens to murder him, monopoly, may be curbed, how his coöperative institutions may reinforce his freedom and render it stable and prolonged. But, having envisaged all this, appreciate that the thing will not be done unless it is inspired by that spirit which made our culture, that spirit in the absence of which our culture will die: and the name of that spirit is the Catholic Church.

The restoration of property must have for its instruments regulations making the dissipation of ownership difficult and the diffusion of ownership easy.

The first in importance of such regulations is the differential tax. With this instrument in hand, Society, if it has the will, can build up again small property in spite of the complexity and centralization of the modern world.

What is needed is a form of tax which not only spares the small man at the expense of his wealthier rival, but actually subsidizes the small man where subsidy is necessary. We have already today differential taxes as between the big man and the small man. The curve of taxation rises steeply with the amount of property possessed, the income attaching·to it, the fortunes which large accumulation leaves at death. But we do not use this advantage for the recreation of economically independent families. We dissipate the revenue so gained in wages and salaries for those in public employment, in usury upon the bank credit to which the modern state is bound. Nothing of the enormous sums gathered by the novel and drastic claims of the State upon large private fortunes goes towards the restoration of property.

It should do so, for the claim of the small-property man is prior to the claim of the state employee. Still more obviously is it prior to the claim of the money lender. The small man will accumulate by natural instinct of self-preservation. He does so in all healthy societies. Such accumulation, such mixture of industry and saving, mark the free peasant everywhere·in the world. At least they so mark him wherever a free peasantry has struck root and established strong traditions.

But there is still a heavy handicap against small savings,

that is, the creation of small capital by accumulation. The sacrifice required for the denial is far greater in the small man than in the large man. The small man foregoes sometimes what are actual necessities, in his effort to attain economic independence. It may be too much for him; as we know, whole classes of Society have given up the effort in despair, rather content to live upon wages controlled by the accumulations of others.

Therefore, if we desire to foster small accumulation, we should subsidize it. We should offer for small investment, especially when that investment is guaranteed by the State, easier opportunities than are offered to the wealthy, and a higher rate of interest. We must be uneconomic and artificial in the affair.

It may be protested that such a reversal of the common competitive arrangements is in contradiction with mere arithmetic. I have myself heard it said, when this reform was proposed, that the funds could not be found whence artifically high interest on small investments could be paid. But those who speak thus are themselves sinning against plain arithmetic. If you examine the statistics of modern state-financing, what you discover is this: The State taxes the community and taxes with especial heaviness the wealthier part of the community, and out of the proceeds of these taxes it pays interest on the loans which it has incurred, the advance of credit by the great banking monopoly which everywhere holds Society by the throat. But the amount which it thus pays to the small bondholders, even where these are very numerous, is insignificant compared with the amounts which it pays to the larger bondholders. A loan subject to, say, 5 percent interest, as were the European loans at the time of the Great War, will pay the full 5 percent interest to the small bondholder, while after payment of taxation by him the larger bondholder will receive only 4 percent or 3 percent.

Were you to differentiate the interest as we now differentiate the taxation, were you to give the small bondholder up to a certain very low limit, 10 percent instead of 5 percent, up to another superior limit 8 percent instead of 10 percent, and so on until the 5 percent level were reached at a point where a still small but respectable accumulation had been created, the equilibrium of your budget would hardly be disturbed, so prodigious is the modern preponderance of large accumulation of capital over small.

It is true that in a society where property was already well distributed, differentiation in favor of the small bondholder would be mathematically impossible. There would be no large bondholders out of whom the fund could come. But as Society now is, in the chief industrial centers, it ought to be self-evident that a hitherto untried principle of differentiating the returns on investment as well as differentiating the tax upon revenue could be undertaken without serious disturbance. Having been undertaken, your bribing of small accumulation would be like the swing which starts an automobile on a cold day. It would set the machinery of small accumulation in motion and rapidly would results grow. Were you paying even as much as 10 percent on the first $500. of accumulation—a proposition which would sound monstrous in the ears of the orthodox today—the extra $50. a year per unit would at first hardly affect the equilibrium of national expenditure. And remember that every advance of this tiny minimum until the level of say $5000. was reached, after which level differentiation by subsidy might cease, would lessen the burden upon the public treasury.

Another reform on the same lines is a differential tax upon transfer. Where the small man sells to the big man or the small unit to the big unit, let there be a high tax upon the transaction, and, the other way about, a low one. For such a system to work, it would be necessary to have a register of property. The property of each citizen or family at such and such intervals of time would have to be set down, but what is the objection to that? It already exists when properties are examined at death. It exists in the English income tax in one large category: what is known as "Schedule A." It exists wherever the property takes the form of registered property in land, and it was the universal rule throughout Society until quite recent times. In the Middle Ages every man's revenue was roughly known, the rental dues paid to this or that office, this or that feudal possession was of common knowledge. If we restored that system today there would be evasion, of course, as there is of every legitimate demand, but the thing as a whole would be sufficiently workable to endure and produce its main effects.

Yet another reform upon the same lines would be a differential tax on every form of movable enterprise. There is nothing in the nature of things which makes the chain store or the big department store a necessity. They have arisen as an evil consequence of an evil principle—the principle of unchecked competition. The departmental store kills the small shopkeeper. The chain store tends to do the same.

The chain store and the departmental store can both be curbed and reduced by differential taxation. A license issued for the carrying on of such and such a business might cost a nominal sum for the first enterprise. If a second of the same kind be added to it in another place, let the second license cost far more. Let the third be so expensive as to be prohibitive, and the thing is done. Put thus, of course, the scheme would be unworkable in its crudity, but with proper attention to details, with elasticity in the rules, the general principle involved could be applied.

It is in fact applied not by the action of the community through taxation, but through the action of the community by public opinion. In many a small unspoiled society today a man having a grocery store in a country town and prospering by his industry and energy does not offend, but the same man setting out to ruin a neighbor in the same line of business does offend; and we can see before our eyes, at any rate in the Old World, that in villages and town units below a certain size, public opinion is effective in preventing the eating up of the small distributor by the larger one. A man's trade is regarded by that public opinion as his livelihood and the taking away of a man's livelihood is not tolerated.

It is clear that the need for such novel and, as it were, artificial experiments is confined to the greater cities and to mechanical production and to exchange. The rules for the better distribution of property under agricultural conditions are the same as regards the differential tax on transfer, but not as regards the differential tax on production. Where a large owner of land and natural forces buys from the small owner, let the transaction be made as expensive as possible; when the transfer is the other way let that transfer be made as easy as possible. But the differential tax upon multiplicity of categories does not apply to the land as it does to the chain store or the big department store.

It will be objected that certain activities necessarily bear a monopolist character. That is true, and on that account the policy with regard to them must be a thing apart and what that policy should be will be later examined. But the inevitability of monopoly is absurdly exaggerated in the modern mind. The great monopolies and quasi-monopolies have come into existence not because they were in the nature of things and unescapable, but because under conditions that restrict competition the smaller unit is heavily handicapped against the larger. Consider the effect of advertisement, for instance. Up to a certain level the effect of advertisement is hardly appreciable. Set up a dozen signs in a large city, and they will affect no one. But after a certain point the effect grows with geometric proportion indeed until it reaches what may be called "saturation." If you put a sign on every building in a large city commanding the citizens, as is the way of advertisers, or even more politely, advising them to buy your soap, not more people will buy it than if you put it up on a quarter of the homes or even a tenth of them. There is a certain limit discoverable in practice after advertisemnt reaches its "optimum." But up to that point the large advertiser has an advantage over the smaller man which increases in geometric proportion.

The moral for those who would preserve or restore small property is evident: impose a differential tax upon advertisement, upon its area and its number and remember that quite apart from the use of such a tax in social reconstruction the horrible exaggeration of modern advertisement is a source of revenue crying out to be taxed. In some communities such taxation is imposed, but it is always ridiculously in favor of the big man against the small one. One of the most remarkable dumb ironies present to the eye today is the receipt stamp which you may discover on any big trade sign in Paris. In the remote corner of some enormous painted advertisement on a wall or hoarding you will discover a tiny square of gummed paper announcing that the advertiser has paid say $10. or $20. to the Treasury, though the advertisement be on a scale which requires for its rental twenty times that sum, and may have for its effect on the revenue of the advertiser a thousand times that sum.

All these points which I have here set down are, of course, tentative. They are suggestions only. They do not pretend to be a program.* What is required is the desire on the part of all sensible reformers to examine every problem in the light of the opportunities it affords for the reëstablishment of the small owner, the economically free man. Hitherto we have worked on the exactly opposite lines. Our modern communities hitherto have left unchecked the natural play of economic forces and of free competition in favor of the big man. Let us reverse engines *in the mind* and change our ideas on what is desirable, let us come to regard the destruction of small property as a disaster and the swelling of large property as a social disease, and the practical remedies will come of themselves.

We may postulate, therefore, this truth: as against Communism, the first alternative reform which those who would preserve civilization must consider, is the better distribution of property. The great quarrel engaged today is a quarrel between the dispossessed and the possessors, or, as it is often put in the destable Victorian jargon, "the haves and the have-nots."

Men are in revolt because the possession and control of the means of production throughout industrial society are in the hands of others than those who do the work of production. They are in revolt because they are divorced from the implements of their trade and because they are exploited for the benefit of others. There are for such a situation only two issues: either to follow the line of least resistance and turn our inhuman Industrial Capitalism into that which it already so closely resembles, an inhuman Communism; or, to put property and the means of production in the hands of those who produce. Not to put it in their control metaphorically, by calling them "The State," but by putting it in their control actually as owners:

---

*I have sketched the general outlines of what might be a political program in the matter. The scheme is to be found in a small book of mine called *The Restoration of Property* (Sheed & Ward).

owners of machines, owners of shares, owners of land and buildings. If and when that is done, Society will be sane and stable again.

Meanwhile it must be emphasized that merely to set things in motion for such an end, even for trying to achieve such an end, is of little purpose unless we safeguard the victory by making the equitable division of property stable. No sane man will want equality of property. No man possessed of some small but sufficient ownership feels any particular enmity to a man possessed of somewhat more. Further, there will always be a tendency to a margin of society where men are not industrious enough or sufficiently self-controlled to preserve their inheritance, however good the safeguards for that inheritance may be. The restoration of property is a sufficient remedy if it applies to a determining number of families in the state making property a habit and giving tone to the whole community.

But, I repeat, we need the extension in time as well as in space. Having achieved a society in which the land and the machine and the stores of goods necessary for production are widely held in several ownerships, we must make that state of affairs permanent or we shall have done nothing.

Now by what set of regulations is this to be done? In some degree, the end is attained by the differential tax where it is easier for the small man to buy from the great than for the great man to buy from the small. Then there is a handicap in favor of small property and against large property.

But there is more needed than that. One must have continuous institutions bolstering up the thing because the thing is not "natural economics." To establish a society the members of which, the component families of which, shall be economically free, is to act against the unchecked tendencies of the world. It is an artificial action like cutting

dykes and raising levees in order to drain what would, left
to itself, be a marsh. You have continually to repair the
levees and to dig out the ditches which drain the fen. Unless you do that the natural conditions return and the
reclaimed land falls back again into bog.

So it is with the maintenance of economic freedom,
that is, well divided property, in any society. Natural economics, that is, men under conditions of drift and unor-
ganized in their own defense, cannot preserve it. Without
special regulations, the larger man will begin eating up
the smaller man and all the evils one has got rid of will
return.

What then are these conservant reguations to be?

When our society was stable and satisfied in the climax
of the Middle Ages, when it was living in a fashion consonant with its right philosophy and human social instincts, the thing was done by laws of hereditary succession.
The holding of the peasant upon the manor as he gradually
emerged from the slave into the serf and from the serf
into the freeman was preserved for him by unbreakable
custom. The son succeeded to the father, the holding
whether large or small paid only such and such dues rigidly
defined, whether in labor or in kind or in cash. The free
tenants could as a rule, especially towards the end of the
Middle Ages, sell their holdings, but there was nearly
always some local duty or some local inducement which
made such sales rare or difficult.

Within the crafts the property of the craftsman in his
house and workshop and in the tools of his trade was
guaranteed by custom. There is always a clause in the rules
given for judicial fines and confiscations. It safeguards
the gear of a farmer, his cattle and horses, wagons and
what not, and is also applicable to the instruments of a
craft. You could not distrain on a man for the things
necessary to his economic independence. Subject to the

difference between modern conditions and medieval conditions in material things, that principle should be revived. But, as we shall see on a later page, the main instrument for the preservation of property in craftsmanship today must be the guild. To render property and the means of production permanent in the industrial field you must revive the guild, incorporate it, and give it powers guaranteed by law.

On parallel lines we must, in any new issue of public bonds, give preference to the small holder thereof.

There is a further regulation which helps to preserve small property, and that is restriction to the power of alienation save within members of a defined group, but on all this I will touch further when I come to the guild. The point to remember is that in any scheme for the reërection of well defined property, there must be included methods for its maintenance as well as for its inception.

In the effort to restore private property as a general institution normal to the family and giving its tone to the whole State, we must remember one very grievous proviso: the task is impossible unless there be still left in the mass of men a sufficient desire for economic independence to urge them towards its attainment. You can give political independence by a stroke of the pen, you can declare slaves to be free or give the vote to men who have hitherto had no vote, but you cannot give property to men or families as a permanent possession unless they desire economic freedom sufficiently to be willing to undertake its burdens.

This consideration has especially affected our political problems in England. Many of our public men, attracted to the idea of diffusing property among many, have discovered that the main obstacle lies in the lack of any desire for such a state of affairs among the wage-earners. They have lived under Capitalism for so long that a secure and sufficient wage is for them the economic ideal.

This reluctance to undertake the responsibilities of ownership appears even in the simple matter of a homestead and it is discoverable not only among the wage-earners, but among the tenant farmers occupied in tilling, or overlooking the tilling, of our land. You will continually find that the English tenant-farmer would rather be under a landlord who can by law turn him out at a year's notice, but must be responsible for the upkeep of his barns and house and enclosures, than be his own master and have to undertake all this business himself. Nor is this only a matter of lack of capital. You will find among us in England any number of men with money laid by which they have put out at interest among their neighbors or into government bonds, but which they will not spend upon the buildings of their farm or upon its main improvements and upkeep.

If this be true, as it is, of a host of our small farmers and still more of the agricultural laborers (whose cottages are rented to them at an uneconomic price—that is, for much less than their cost would warrant), it is still more true of the wage-earner in the towns. He has now lived so long—for some three lifetimes—under the wage conditions of our great industrial cities that he neither knows of nor desires any other. Make his livelihood secure either by a legal fixed wage or by State subsidy in place of it and he is content. He is not and does not desire to be an economically free citizen.

It is true that Great Britain is an extreme case and that at her very doors the Irishman acts in an exactly contrary manner. He is determined on the ownership of his own land, and at vast sacrifices he has achieved it. In his case, the determination to be an economically free man was so strong that he struggled for a century against the heaviest adverse conditions and at last achieved his end, even compelling the Bank of England, which lies behind the whole of our credit system, to finance the repurchase of his land from those who had confiscated it generations ago, mainly on the excuse of religion. The repurchase of Irish land from the large owners (who were in the main the descendants of the foreign grantees of Irish soil) was effected in what is called the Wyndham Act by the issue of interest-bearing bonds under the guarantee of English credit—that is, virtually the Bank of England. The usury as it fell due was to be paid by the former tenants and these gradually bought up the land until it should fall after many such payments into the full ownership of the occupier.

The political fortunes of this scheme have their own interest, but only slightly concern our subject. The instalments payable on the land were duly received by the former great landowners through the agency of the British government. There came a moment when the Irish people refused to transfer the money to England and kept it in the hands of their own government, whence arose a quarrel not yet appeased. Anyhow the point to notice is that because there existed in Ireland this strong demand for ownership on the part of the peasantry, ownership was achieved, and because such a desire does not exist in England, ownership is there not achieved and is not in process of achievement.

There was, indeed, a considerable purchase of land by English tenants immediately following on the Great War, but this was artificial and has come to nothing.

What happened was this: agricultural prices were exceptionally high on account of the scarcity produced by the European upheaval. The profits on the tilling of the land were correspondingly great. The governing class had, through Parliament, which is its instrument, made ambiguous promises that this state of things should be bolstered up. Meanwhile the principal landowners, who are the members of that class and who were well advised that the artificial condition could not last, offered the land to their tenants. These had not the capital wherewith to pay immediately, they borrowed credit from the banks; when the transfer was accomplished the upshot of it was that the banking monopoly, with the Bank of England, of course, at its root, stood in the shoes of the old landowners. But the class of free peasants owning their own small farms was further than ever from coming into existence. There are no full statistics of the movement. Anyone attempting even to make a rough estimate of what happened in this considerable economic change finds his investigation hampered at every turn by the complexities of conveyance and registration and the secrecy in which most of the transactions are kept. But the broad fact is notorious. Some very large proportion of English agricultural land changed hands in the third decade of the 20th century. Nominally, the transfer was from the old large landlords to a new class of independent small proprietors. Actually, the transfer was from the old large landlords to the banking monopoly, which is in Great Britain the most stable of institutions and the best organized in the world.

In the attempt to provide a human and satisfactory alternative to Communism as a solution for our modern ills which Capitalism has produced, the second division is the control of monopoly.

The capitalist system born of competition has ended in the very contradiction of that principle. It used to be preached in defense of the capitalist system that by its fundamental doctrine of free competition, production was rendered more efficient, necessaries and all other goods were made cheaper, and indirectly the whole commonwealth thus benefited. The Capitalist in the early stages of Capitalism did not intend to benefit his fellow beings, he intended to benefit no one but himself. That was the very foundation of his creed. But in practice, it was argued, by leaving his love of gain free play he would indirectly be the benefactor of all.

For a long time there seemed to be something to be said for so strange a paradox. Turn greed loose among men and general content and happiness due to abundance will be the result. Leave men to prey without restraint upon their fellow beings and the mass would not suffer from the rapacity thus let loose, but, on the contrary, benefit from it. Thus a railway would be built between two towns by a group of Capitalists. Another group would build an alternative route, the two would compete and their competition would lower the rates to a minimum. At the same time it would lead to every kind of discovery for the betterment of communications, the machinery of transport would continually improve, and so forth.

Give full license to any distributor of goods, say a grocer, to undercut the competitor at will, to fix his own prices, even at the ruin of a neighbor smaller than himself, and in the long run you would produce a more efficient, a stronger, a better public service. For quite a lifetime all this apparently held true, but the inevitable happened; greed thus let loose produced monopoly. The large producers and the large distributors made mergers among themselves, or, failing that, established agreements in the restriction of competition. Prices were fixed between them and these monopolies, once established, became the masters of the community.

Their mastery is now quite patent and admitted. It is not universal. A very large field of competition remains, affecting considerable units and even in small businesses a certain measure of vitality has survived, but the tendency to monopoly is continually at work, monopoly continually advances, and it is clear that if the process be not checked we should end in no very long space of time by the great mass of production, distribution, and exchange falling into the control of comparatively few men who would thus be necessarily the masters of the community. As it is, the private citizen is already helpless against these controls in the larger part of his activities. The great bulk of what he must purchase, he must purchase at a price, and, what is worse, after a fashion and according to a design laid down for him by others. Demand no longer controls supply in most activities of life, rather does supply order and enregiment demand.

It may be said that in part this is due to mass production and the use of machinery with that object. This is true, but more important is the action of the whole on monopoly. "Competition has done its work," you will hear thinking men say on all sides, especially those who are content with the upshot of the affair. And if there be no further development and no change-over to the control of monopoly by public powers, not only will competition have done its work and have ceased, but its successor, monopoly, will be the master of the commonwealth.

Another way of putting this was that set of phrases common upon the lips of Socialists a generation ago, to which allusion has already been made—"Let the big businesses grow, the nearer they become to monopolies the more easily shall they be taken over by the State." The idea of Socialism arose, as we have seen, through the conception of all monopolies merging in one great monopoly, that of the State.

The defenders of economic liberty, who are also necessarily the defenders of private property as a principle, dreaded and combated this result. But they did nothing to stop it. For by their own theory as it was propounded in the capitalist age, they had to defend competition and in so defending it, defended that which would inevitably lead to monopolist control at last.

Therefore, when it was proposed that public law should put some check upon the growth of monopoly, a cry against government interference was raised in the name of freedom. The more intelligent of those who raised this cry knew very well that the prevention of common action against monopoly by the State would work in their favor alone. They used the principle that the State should interfere as little as possible, but they used it in order that they should acquire for themselves such political and economic power as it was the business of Society to prevent. Meanwhile the old-fashioned economist, living in the traditions of the past, continued to denounce State interference, which he confused with that Socialism it was his business to combat.

The strange alliance between these two ill assorted allies, the old-fashioned liberal and the modern monopolist, resulted in the prodigious growth of the latter until today he is in every department, but especially in transport and finance, a master.

Now it is imperatively necessary, if well divided property is to come into existence again and to be maintained, that monopoly should be dealt with according to two main principles which we must bear clearly in mind.

The first principle is this: everything must be done to check the growth of monopoly, to interfere at the beginning of its appearance and to disperse its forces. In so far as this can be done by voluntary coöperation among the citizens let it be thus done, but seeing what the power of wealth is, especially in our modern urban communities and more particularly through the control of the Press, voluntary coöperation can have no such effect as the action of the State. Let State action—that is, let laws or guild regulations supported by the power of the State—prevent the beginnings of monopoly wherever it may appear and make such arrangements that it cannot grow.

The second principle is this: where monopoly is inevitable, there let State control and even, where necessary, State ownership, take the place of private control and private ownership. A Socialist of the old school, the leader of his party in Belgium, said half a lifetime ago: "Since monopoly is inevitable, let it be taken over by the commonwealth lest we all become the servants of a few rich men." There was a truth in this but it was a half truth. Monopoly is not inevitable in itself, it is inevitable only under certain conditions. Men often talk as though it were an inevitable product of machinery or rapidity of communication or what not. That is an error typical of the time in which we live, a time in which men have forgotten the truth and function of free will and in which, on the parallel of popular scientific materialism, it is imagined that human society must follow rigidly the force of things, undetermined by human choice. Men see monopoly existing all round them and growing every day. They take it for granted that there is therefore no choice in the matter, that we must submit to the evil and bear it as best we can.

Now, no monopoly is inevitable; not even the most apparently obvious. No monopoly comes into existence save by the acceptation of those who submit to it. A monopoly is often cheaper and more precise and accurate in its working, and more rapid as well, than would be a number of competing or partly competing units. It may, therefore, be chosen by the consumers of its product in preference to the product of lesser units. But there is no monopoly which either public opinion or direct action of government cannot destroy if we are willing to pay the price. For instance, that most obvious of all monopolies, the national mail system. If for some reason men could not tolerate the monopolist power of that one function they could do without it. Their mail would be delivered much less regularly and less swiftly—that is the price they would have to pay—but it is not true to say that the monopoly is inevitable. A law or the separate action of free men could destroy it. That is true of every monopoly under the sun and of every tendency to monopoly.

In practice, however, monopoly does come into existence especially under modern conditions. Some monopolies have existed from the beginning of human society. For instance, the monopoly of main communication throughout any one society. There is no society so primitive but that its roadways or tracks must be kept up. And though it leave each petty unit—parish or township or what not—to keep up a section of tracks or roads, there must be some coördinating authority however simple, otherwise continuity of communication would break down. One cannot leave it to a local man to repair a bridge, for instance, at his own good pleasure. If one did that he could hold up the community or even by mere laziness destroy its transport.

In a highly complex society, such as ours has become today, the examples of what may be called "natural monopoly" greatly increase in number. There can be a certain amount of competition, for instance, between various groups of railroads, but our transport would become impossible if a great number of these acted in mere competition and independence one of another. Again, there are a large number of activities where the concentration of control in one center makes the cost of production so enormously cheaper than the cost of production as it would be in many small centers, that the tendency to concentration is overwhelming.

The major example of this in modern times is, of course, the centralization and monopoly of bank credit, on which under modern conditions much the most of production, distribution, and exchange depends. It is true there are societies in which the creation of bank credit is much freer than in others. It is most centralized and most an absolute monopoly in Great Britain, on which account British banking is the most efficient in the world and also the most tyrranic. Where the creation of bank credit is permitted to a large number of independent centers, the instability of the banking system must evidently be greater. Where it is, as in England, virtually under one central control, its stability is at a maximum. Now of all monopolies, this one—that of bank credit— most urgently demands public control. Unless public authority is the master of that particular force, that force will be the master of the community. Society will fall into that worst of all conditions—not worse for order but worse for its ultimate fate and its morals—power divorced from responsibility. We have had in the capital field of foreign policy a major example of this during the last few years. It is an example which everybody should mark, especially as it has been carefully hidden.

Great Britain went to war in order to prevent the German Reich from building a fleet that could rival her own. After the war the Victors' Alliance, which included Great Britain, laid it down that the Reich of the future should have no fleet worth calling a fleet. It was from the point of view of Great Britain the chief fruit of the common victory. But the Reich was kept in being principally by the support of Great Britain, because it was thought to be on land a counterbalance to the land power of France, and it has been and must be the permanent policy of Great Britain to keep the land forces of the Continent divided and in rivalry.

So far so good. The Bank of England, and with it those who control the issue of bank credit from England, saw in the impoverishment and exhaustion of the Reich

through war and defeat an opportunity for placing great
loans at enormously high interest. It was taken for granted
on the experience of the past and without considering the
complete change of conditions produced by the Great
War, that a promise to pay by any considerable modern
government was equivalent to actual security for payment.
Every effort was made by the Bank of England—and most
successfully made—to prevent the occupation of German
territory as a guarantee for the payment of reparations.
It never occurred to the money lenders—more accurately
the credit lenders—that, unless they occupied territory
they would have no security for repayment of the vast
usury which they expected on the advances made. To take
but one example out of a great number: the City of Berlin
borrowed from London at 10 percent for municipal purposes. The 10 percent was really more like 12 when all
the frills and commissions had been allowed for. The
usurers did not doubt for a moment that the promise of
the City of Berlin to pay $12. a year for every $100. worth
of credit extended would be kept. In the past, such payments had always been made by Great Powers and when
lesser countries defaulted they were as a rule coerced
by the fleets and armies at the disposal of the lenders.

We all know what happened. In a very short time the
Germans refused to pay the interest while keeping the
material goods and services which were the product of
the credit extended to them. One of the main uses to which
they put this advantage which had been given them with
such enormous lack of judgment by the English banking
monopoly was to set about building a new fleet. Today
the taxpayer of Great Britain has to find usury on vast
new sums of credit extended to Germans by his own
English banking monopoly in order that the Germans
may build a new fleet. The Englishman has to pay all
right; the banking monopoly is sure of its money in *his*

case; but the German loans have gone down the wind. They will never be recovered.

The whole thing is perhaps the most signal example of the stupidity of mammon which history can afford. First the English people are burdened with taxation beyond all known precedent in order to destroy a rival fleet; the wealthier citizens are mulcted of, all told (counting death duties and income tax and every form of impost) between half and three quarters of their fortunes, of which sums a great proportion goes to usury on the credits of the Great War: and now a further proportion is to go in usury on credits provided to meet a rival whom the English have themselves re-armed! That example is taken from foreign policy and is so glaring that no other is needed. But the power of monopoly and financial control is not confined to foreign policy. You find it in every detail of the national life. Bank credit granted or withheld makes or unmakes any enterprise, bank credit being naturally attracted towards large enterprise rather than small, supports the growth of the large unit against the small one and makes for the continual increase of that ill distribution of property which is our main modern political and social evil.

Now of all monopolies the financial monopoly is that which most naturally comes into being, and, having once done so, is most difficult for any power but that of the government itself to master. It is the most natural to come into being because it is a field in which the large unit most easily swallows up the small and in which communication is easiest. You can transfer millions of bank credit from one end of the world to the other, by a few cable words. You can create and put into action a mass of bank credit in, say, Yokohama, at the will of a small group of men in, say, Paris or the City of London at a moment's notice. Such fluidity does not apply to any other form of economic activity.

But the strongest motive for the control of this monopoly by the State still remains the power of that monopoly to control the State itself unless the State determines to be its own master and to make financial credit its servant. You will never have safeguard for well divided property nor for the freedom of economic activity in Society until central credit is controlled by the officers of the whole community.

We have seen that modern conditions do make for the growth of monopoly if not inevitably, yet certainly by very strong tendencies. But when all these are allowed for, it remains true that the bulk of modern monopoly or quasi-monopoly is not the result of always irresistible economic forces but simply the result of leaving great bodies of wealth free to attack and destroy lesser units.

We all know what the weapons are which the greater units can use for the destruction of its lesser rival. We have already seen how much more proportionally effective is an advertisement in the hands of the greater unit. Up to a certain degree of enlargement all overhead charges are reduced by concentration under one control. The actual instruments used are often proportionally less expensive on a large scale than on a small—and so on.

But the most effective of all weapons in the hands of large units—and the most immoral—is the weapon of underselling. When there is no fixed price, when therefore, the controller of a particular unit of production or distribution can present his goods at a temporary loss, he can by so doing kill the lesser unit, which cannot stand the strain. A large unit with a reserve of capital and credit $10x$ can go on putting goods before the consumer at a loss five times as long as the smaller unit whose measure of capital and credit is $2x$. The greater rival will have killed the lesser rival but only one-fifth of that greater rival's resources have been used.

There are lesser subsidiary forces at work to create monopoly in this fashion. For instance, a large unit can gather information on a wider field, it can coördinate that information better, it can afford to scrap out-of-date material better than can the smaller unit—and all the rest of it.

Now for the prevention of this evil, the growth of monopoly, whether the production or distribution through the unchecked play of the larger unit against the smaller, there is but one effective instrument. It was the instrument discoverable in the very origins of Society and proved by our fathers in the Middle Ages, only destroyed when the social philosophy of Catholic times was ousted by a false social philosophy following on the Reformation: and that instrument is the GUILD.

The guild is that instrument whereby any form of human economic activity can work corporately and yet, at the same time, with the recognition of human economic activity—that is human dignity and the function of human free will.

The essential of the guild-idea is that men pursuing the same form of activity, but only in coöperation limited to the end of preserving the economic freedom—that is the property and livelihood—of each member of the guild.

The function of the guild is not to prevent a man from prospering in some economic activity wherein he shows merit and industry; its function is to prevent the man so prospering from taking away the economic basis of one or more of his fellows for his own advantage.

The function of the guild is not to support the guildsman in a war against the rest of Society or in struggling against some other section of Society: it is to strengthen the guildsman as an individual and as the head of that unit of all Society—the family—so that he may hold his own against the threat of too heavy a competition from his fellows or of oppression by economic activities external to his own.

Where the economic activity of a guild requires instruments of a certain cost the guild sees to it that those instruments are not gathered up into the control of a few hands. Where that competition is necessary it is the business of the guild to supervise the arrangement of it and to see that under it the lesser man is not destroyed by the greater man. It is also the function of the guild to fix prices for the guild product, lest the guild should exploit unduly its fellow citizens outside its own jurisdiction. Lastly, the guild must, as I have said, defend its own corporation against the undue pressure of other corporations. The guild itself is but one member of a commonwealth of guilds, as it were, the network of which should cover any well organized state in which men aim at founding and preserving economic freedom for the individual and the family.

These are abstract principles. Let us put them in concrete form for the sake of giving them substance. There are a number of grocers in the community. If these grocers and their businesses are organized in a guild, the guild will set a limit to the business which any one grocer can do. It need not be a very rigid limit. There is certainly no necessity here for equality, which, we can repeat here as throughout all our examination of economic conditions, is neither feasible nor by the mass of men desired in economic affairs. But the guild would set a limit such that the least of its members should at least have a livelihood. It would forbid any one of its members even the most prosperous from threatening the livelihood of lesser guildsmen.

In the guild system there could not take place, for instance, the spectacle which I have before my own eyes in London. In that town there exists a respectable and important grocery business which the same family has conducted for three generations. It supplies a certain restricted but fairly well-to-do neighborhood, has provided a good and slowly increasing income for those who manage it. One of these combinations called in America "chain stores," finding this private-family grocery business supplying the locality, bought up a property *next door* to it, set up one of the innumerable grocery units in their possession, and proceeded to undersell the old established shop in order to drive it out of business.

That sort of thing is going on all over our country and probably all over yours. It is incidental to the chaotic economic condition in which we live, and if no control is established it will end by destroying family businesses altogether. Now under a guild system that would be impossible. A man could not open a grocery shop unless he were an accepted member of the guild, for the guild would be chartered by law for its members to pursue certain activities which would be legally forbidden to those not members of the guild. He could not undersell because within certain limits prices and profits would be fixed by the guild. He could not even wantonly and maliciously set up competition at the very doors of another guildsman for that would bring him before the court of the guild which would forbid such action.

Take another instance. A man requires for his carpenter shop certain instruments to the value of, say $2000. Another larger concern dealing perhaps with a more complicated form of product will want a shop the instruments wherein are worth say $4000. Another smaller man will require only $1000. of such capital. There comes along a discovery which permits some particular kind of carpentry work to be done much better and more quickly and more cheaply by a new instrument, but that instrument costs $50,000. It is beyond the means of any one individual guildsman. The guild as a corporation provides it, oversees its use and the distribution of its product among the guilds-men in proportion to their standing within the guild. The guild has already seen to it that no one guildsman shall be so great as to destroy the livelihood of another. The productive property among the guildsmen, though not equally distributed, is at least sufficiently distributed for each to be an owner, and now, according to their assessment as guildsmen, they share in the product of the new instrument.

Take another instance—a unit in which little movable property is required—a guild of lawyers or doctors, for instance. It will make rules forbidding certain forms of competition which it regards as dangerous to the independence of its members. We have already in most professions rules of this kind existing as customs enforced by the opinion and coöperation of members of the profession. Let such rules be chartered and legally enforceable, and the full professional guild will come into existence.

It would be easy to fill the whole of such pages as these with nothing but the consideration of this fruitful, elementary, and essential economic structure. Our ancestors enjoyed it for centuries; it was the prime economic institution of the State; relics of its still existing among us testify to its value (for instance, the Waterman's Guild of the River Thames in London). In our efforts at economic reform, which shall recover for Society its health and content, the formation of the guild is essential.*

In conclusion let us emphasize the four marks of the guild. Each of them is vital to its existence, each necessary,

---

* The reader may consult the works of the late Mr. Penty on this subject. They are lucid, thorough, and illuminating, especially where they deal with the *Just Price* as established by the guild.

and each workable when men are once accustomed to the idea and to its practice.

The first principle is this: the guild must be self-governing, making its own rules, admitting members on terms which it itself devises, fixing the price of their products of activities, judging the work done so it does not fall below a certain standard, forming arrangements whereby corporate action by many guildsmen may be undertaken where something needs to be done which is beyond the means of the individual guildsman. This character of self-government should include some central meeting place for office works and for the intercommunion of members, and a system of these centers could be established, nationwide.

The second principle is that the guild like any other living organism must be limited. The numbers which may practise within it must in the first instance be decided by the self-governing guild itself—that is the governing organs and officers of the guild. But only in conjunction with the authorities responsible for the whole State, otherwise a guild might use its monopoly to the prejudice of Society around it. There is never a danger of such limited and privileged bodies becoming too large—the danger is always of their becoming too small, and therefore the State must have the power to revise the numbers of each in order that the needs of Society may be satisfied. The same rule applies to the prices fixed by the guild. For the general good of Society there must be some central social authority which will decide where the guild by its set of prices is unduly exploiting the community.

The third principle is that of property. A guild must of its very nature be a guild of owners. The individual and the family are otherwise deprived of that very economic freedom which it is the object of the guild to maintain. A guild organized on a communistic basis is a contradiction in terms.

Supposing, for instance, you have a general transport guild divided into numerous branches. Supposing one of the branches is the guild operating such and such a railroad. Your individual guildsmen or their families would not own, the one a locomotive, the other a truck, a third a depot. The thing has only to be stated to show its absurdity. But the stock in the affair should be owned by the members thereof. Where in the nature of things (and a railway is an example of that) the unit is large, self-government is proportionally difficult and the measure of State administration in the control must be proportionally larger. Yet the element of self-government can be actively present. The various branches of activities in a railway system should each have its departmental charter, meeting, voting distribution and the rest, with central organs for the supervision and coöperation of the whole corporation.

The fourth principle is perhaps the most important of all. If we are to prevent the arising of a proletariat, which evil it is the whole object of the guild to prevent, we must have hierarchy. Hierarchy is essential to all human affairs anyhow. It is as essential to the management of a guild as to the management of any other social organism. There must be hierarchy of office and of duties. But in the particular function of the guild and particularly of the craft guild you must have either hierarchy in the sense of a distinction between the postulant and the admitted member.

That is the conception underlying the ancient and invaluable institution called apprenticeship. By it the guild is renewed, its continuity maintained, and not only its continuity but its excellence, its aptitude in doing the work for which it exists. The guildsman naturally desires his son, or, if the activities of the guild are expanding, then two or more of his sons, to enjoy the priviliges of freedom and ownership which he has himself enjoyed. He proposes them as postulants—that is, as young men envisaging full membership in the guild. In that class and with that character they are admitted. They are subject to the authority of the superiors trained in the work, and only after admission to full competency given their full degree. The old term for that last state was "Master." Thus as the individual members die off they are renewed, the organism as a whole continually reproduces itself, and its aptitude for its function is guaranteed.

The guild cannot be restored, of course, upon a fixed program. No human thing can thus be brought into existence mechanically. It must feel its way into existence once more as it did when it was first formed in the earliest ages of mankind and particularly when it was at its highest and most useful—in the Middle Ages. But the idea is so consonant to man and so obvious a need of our present distracted economic society, that it has only to be stated and vigorously preached to make headway.

Conversion

Even when one has most fully considered in its details the policy required for the restoration of property, and of consequent economic freedom as an alternative to Communism, there remains a qualification or proviso attaching to that policy. It is of such a fundamental character that it determines the whole. Lacking it, the policy is certainly foredoomed to failure; recollecting it and working upon it, and only so, the policy may succeed.

That proviso or qualification is the reëstablishment in our midst of the Catholic culture and for that purpose the advancement, up to and beyond a certain necessary minimum limit, of Catholic numbers and practice in the community. So much being said, let me define the terms of this proposition.

In the first place, a conversion to the Catholic culture is necessary to the restoration of economic freedom because economic freedom was the fruit of that culture in the past. The guild, the coöperative agricultural system, the whole network of safeguards for family property— all these things which we have seen in the past and propose as a program for the future—came out of the Catholic culture which was itself the product of Catholic doctrine.

It was the Faith which gradually and indirectly transformed the slave into the serf, and the serf into the free peasant. It was the Faith which took the guild, inherited from the Pagan Empire, and set it up for the foundational thing it was during all the great medieval period: the guarantee of freedom. It was the Faith which by its moral atmosphere checked and curbed usury—that usury whereby Pagan Society, before the triumph of the Church, had been thoroughly sapped and which today is sapping us again. It was the Faith which put competition within its bounds and made its limited practice subservient to general well divided property, where its excess would have divided Society into very many destitute and few possessors. It was the disruption of Catholic unity in Europe which let in all the evils from the extreme of which we now suffer and are in peril of dissolution.

We cannot build up a society synthetically, for it is an organic thing; we must see to it first that the vital principle is there from which the characters of the organism will develop. You will not be able to set up in a pagan or an heretical or a wholly indifferent society the institutions characteristic of economic freedom; you will not be able to curb competition which alone would be sufficient to destroy such freedom nor pursue permanently and consecutively any one part of the program. The thing must be done as a whole and it can be done as a whole only by the ambient influence of Catholicism.

Briefly we must begin by aiming at the conversion of Society, failing which no scheme of stable economic freedom will stand. We came, remember, out of slavery; our society was once wholly based on slavery and to slavery it is returning. As a defense against such a decline there is none but the general counter-action of Catholicism.

So much for the first point; the second point is this: A Catholic culture does not mean or imply universality. A nation or a whole civilization is of the Catholic culture not when it is entirely composed of strong believers minutely practising their religion, nor even when it boasts a majority of such, but when it presents *a determining number* of units—family institutions, individuals, inspired by and tenacious of the Catholic spirit.

This doctrine of the determining number has already appeared in these pages. It is essential to the comprehension of any political and social movement, and must first be clearly grasped before we proceed to the further points of method in Conversion.

The determining number in any matter is discovered by experience and inspection; it is not arrived at by any mathematical rule. For instance, in the case of rare events, a very small number would be sufficient to have a determining effect. A district in which there falls every ten years or so a violent earthquake is a district in which earthquakes take place in a determining number. The whole time occupied by shocks in a century, if you added it up, together would perhaps come to less than an hour; yet without doubt some island known to be subject to such exceptional catastrophies though only once every few years for a few minutes at a time would be an island regarded by all men as exceptionally cursed with this kind of misfortune. A particular street in a city where half a dozen murders occurred in the course of a year and then again in the course of the following year, and so on, would be notorious; it would reek of murder, though the total number of homes involved might not even be five percent of the total inhabiting the street.

At the other extreme, where you are dealing with things normal to a man in every situation of life, a determining number connotes a very large proportion of the community. We call a society negroid only when a very large proportion of African blood is present. Even in things which are not normal to man, which are not to be expected of men everywhere, such as racial characteristics, but particular habits general to a society, this rule obtains. The determining number must be a large one—how large only experience and inspection can decide. Nor will it ever be an exact number but always something lying between certain limits.

Again, the determining number can only apply to categories wherein the majority are accessible to the matter concerned. For instance, a society in which most adult men and women are or have been married is a society in which marriage as an institution presents itself in a determining number. A very large proportion of the community will be below the age of marriage; there will be many bachelors and spinsters, many widowers and many widows, but experience will soon discover whether marriage be or be not the characteristic institution of that society.

In the case of a religion, or rather of a religious atmosphere, the prime condition of the determining number is that it should impose its texture or color upon Society as a whole. It is probable that in the greater part of the Middle Ages the greater part of men in the greater part of Christendom practised their religion imperfectly or not at all. But there was no corresponding negative influence; the positive influence radiating from those who were intensely practising to an outer fringe among whom practice had decayed even to extinction, gave to the England, France, Spain, Germany and Italy of the time a character wholly Catholic.

These things being so, what are the methods by which we may attempt the task of restoring this general Catholic atmosphere to the modern world?

Let us begin with estimating the forces opposed to us and the forces in our favor. Those forces differ according to whether we are considering a nation of ancient Catholic culture such as France today, divided upon religion; or one of those nations which broke away from the Catholic unity at the moment of the Reformation. Or again, one of those nations such as Holland, in which, while the government and most of the wealth is non-Catholic or anti-Catholic, there is a very large minority—soon perhaps to be one-half—of Catholic citizens. There is also a separate case altogether, to which you yourselves in the United States belong: the nation which was founded and grew up from a moment when the disruption of Christendom had long taken place; the nation which had at its origins an overwhelmingly predominant anti-Catholic or non-Catholic tradition and social habit—later modified by Catholic immigration.

The forces working for Catholic restoration and against Catholic restoration are very different both in character and proportion in these various forms of Society.

In the nations of old and continuous Catholic culture, of which France may be taken as the leading example, Society is now divided somewhat sharply into the Catholic and non-Catholic; but the anti-Catholic derives its tradition not from the Reformation but from direct reaction against Catholic discipline and authority. It is not hostile to traditional Catholic morals; on the contrary, it is, even when it least knows it, steeped in Catholic philosophy and its direct results; but it *is* in active rebellion against the discipline of the Church and has abandoned faith in her primary doctrines—even that of immortality, and latterly even that of one creative God.

This antagonism is generally called in the nations of Catholic culture by the name of "anti-clericalism." Properly this name belongs rather to a political attitude which watches with jealousy and suspicion any excess of power of the clergy in civil and political matters, but in practice it has come to mean the distinction between the anti-Catholic in the nations of Catholic culture, and his fellow citizen who whether personally practising or not, leans by sympathy towards the Catholic Church and all its traditions.

In the nations which broke away in the 16th century, notably in Prussia* and England, which are the two great examples of Protestantism, the dislike and hatred of Catholicism varies in degree from one to another; but the hatred and ignorance are commonly allied. Great Britain is the country where the dislike of Catholic things is the strongest, and where at the same time the memory of them has most thoroughly died out. In the Germanies and even in Prussia proper there is a great knowledge of Catholicism, both because that society is attached to historical learning, and because something like one half of the German race retained the Faith, so that the common language and whole body of social habit is shared by Catholic and non-Catholic alike.

Both these divisions in Europe have this in common,

---

* I am here using the word "Prussia" to mean old Prussia, before the annexation of the Rhineland. The Rhenish provinces of the Reich are, of course, in the main Catholic; they are not attached by their traditions to Prussia proper, centered in Berlin, which capital and district is and has been for centuries the continental pole of anti-Catholicism.

that either was founded and formed by the Catholic Church in the Middle Ages; those who broke away from Catholic unity still preserve some memory, and many ruins, of their Catholic past; those who did not break away are, even where the anti-Catholic feeling is strongest, fully conscious of the Catholic past, between which and themselves there is no breach of continuity.

When we are dealing with the New World and in particular with the United States we come across a completely different state of affairs. From the beginning of this society the State or community was Protestant in character; it was at first overwhelmingly so; later that condition was modified, but this was accounted for by immigration much more than by any other factor, and the Catholic immigrants were poor.

Now in the history of all nations the control of wealth profoundly affects the development of the social world. The ownership of the land and of the reserves of wealth, the control, that is, of capital and therefore of industry, lay in the main with the families of Protestant descent, English, Scottish and some Dutch. These continued to give the tone to the commonwealth. Apart from that, the numerical position of Catholics in the mass of Society was always inferior. There was a whole lifetime during which it rapidly grew; but the Catholics were still a minority living in the midst of a society the general tone of which derived from the Reformation and in a large degree from Calvinism.

These divisions exist; they modify, as I have said, the nature and the proportion of the forces working for and against a general restoration of the Catholic culture. Thus in one society the forces of nationalism (as in England) will be fiercely opposed to such a restoration; while elsewhere (as in France) the force of nationalism, once semi-hostile, is now upon the whole favorable to a restoration of the Catholic air. But of every modern society of whatever complexion within our civilization, certain main forces appear hostile and unfavorable to that recovery of the Catholic atmosphere, without which our culture must perish.

There is in favor of our restoration the whole volume of history; the myths and falsehoods of official history whether anti-clerical in Catholic countries or nationalist-Protestant in others, are opposed to us, but the whole body of historical truth is with us. It is an historical truth which has only to be examined to be admitted, that our civilization was made by the Catholic Church and that its fullness and sanity have depended upon the maintenance of the Catholic framework.

Similarly there are opposed to us a number of irrational associations of ideas, such as the association of ideas between anti-Catholicism and the cause of social justice, or the association between the progress of physical science and the progress of scepticism. In that department, as in the department of history, knowledge is on our side; all that we have to combat is ignorance. Therefore we hold trump cards. But the strength of the trumps we hold is the consonance between Catholic morals (the fruit of Catholic doctrine) and the discoverable nature of man. Men can pragmatically discover that through the Faith human things return. Their despair in the absence of the Faith is the strongest asset we have.

Opposed to our effort in countries mainly anti-Catholic by tradition (and with these alone we are here dealing—countries founded and governed by men who were born out of contact with the Catholic Church and largely hostile to it by tradition) are two forces so different that it is a puzzle to connect them; yet one does find them acting together: the force of ignorance and the force of distaste. It might seem more rational that one should hate only what one knows, or even dislike only what one knows; but in point of fact men often particularly dislike something of which they know very little.

The reason would seem to be that men hate mainly through one particular contact. Thus, though of the innumerable facets of the human character, we come across in some person but one, and that one distasteful, we may well conceive a dislike for the whole character, through that one most imperfect experience. So it is with the attitude of the non-Catholic world towards the Catholic Church. They will find themselves in reaction against the strong organization of the Church, the unfamiliar external "clothing" of the Church, its liturgy in an ancient tongue, its ornaments, and what not; very often they find themselves in reaction against its claim to authority. More often still against its alien or cosmopolitan manner, contrasting with their own narrower national traditions. But whatever the explanation, the main fact we have to consider in approaching our problem is the combination of ignorance and dislike. We are attempting to extend the Catholic atmosphere over multitudes who in varying degrees know not, and dislike, the Faith. We aim at permeating with Catholic culture the whole Society, the culture of which is still both unfamiliar with, and hostile to, that culture.

It is clear that in such an effort the method to be pursued and the instruments to be used will be very different from those to which men turn in a country of ancient Catholic tradition. In the one, still an existing and strong, an active philosophy has to be reinforced until it shall again permeate the social mind; that is the way one has to work, for instance, in France or among the intellectual middle class in Italy, or among the desperate and angry proletarian population of the Spanish towns.

But with societies of Protestant origin and type it is otherwise; how are we to set to work there?

As it seems to me, the strategy required may be summed up in two titles: Print and Program.

It behooves us to make the Church known, her doctrines, her whole spirit, her past—the thing itself, the personality—by the medium of Print. And it behooves us to give body to our effort, to provide it with a concrete end, to sustain it with a conscious task, by presenting a Program (in politics they call it a "Platform") wherein may be discovered a solution for the grave, the now almost mortal, ills which Society is suffering because of an original abandonment of the Faith.

It may here be objected that I am talking of very base and material things, or at least of temporal things. That is true of the method and of the instruments I here propose. The conversion of any society or of the world for that matter, is the work of Grace, and in so far as men are the agents of Grace it is the work of example; it is Martyrs and Saints who will reintroduce the Faith, in so far as it can be restored. But I am here speaking only of particular and circumscribed action, because I am speaking of a practical method towards a practical end.

Let us take these two terms in their order; and first the use of Print, before turning to the idea of a Program. Print is an unsatisfactory, because of a most imperfect, method of communicating our ideas to our fellowmen. Especially is it unsatisfactory through its imperfection when the ideas to be conveyed have all the magnitude and multiplicity of that which is the greatest, most diverse and yet most united of all conceptions, the Faith. The true instrument for the general propagation of the Faith, that is, the true social instrument as distinguished from the personal instrument of example, is predication: action by word of mouth. It was the method by which the Church was founded; it is the method by which the Faith has been maintained through the long centuries of its action. But as things are here and now, our main available method is the printing press. Through it only do we reach the multitude. Through it in the main must we reach the mass of men. Predication still plays its part, especially in discussion with our fellows; and more particularly when a discussion or lecture or any other form of predication is addressed to those who are not of us. But upon the Press must we concentrate for our chief effort; and by it in the main shall we succeed or fail.

Now the appeal of print falls into two very different groups, as things are now organized. There is first the appeal of the book; there is next the appeal of the ephemeral press, the daily papers, the magazines and reviews. To work through the latter is to work under a very heavy handicap; the Faith is not "news"; the public approaches an article in a magazine or newspaper or review with the object of receiving information on things the appeal of which is already familiar to them, it desires to hear of travel and tragedy, of comedy, of personalities rendered famous or notorious by the events of the day. On this account, unfortunately, the mass of Catholic action aiming at Catholic effect upon one's fellowmen is canalized into publications already earmarked, as it were, for an audience already Catholic. It even gets to be canalized into publications dealing particularly with what may be called the domestic activities of the Church, its services, its orders, its affairs "of the household." And the affairs of the household are tedious or meaningless to those not of the household. We must, of course, use the ephemeral press to the best of our power; it reaches a hundred readers where the book reaches one. The one avenue of approach which we have through the Press and which is of some value here is notices written of books, the comments issued to the public by reviewers, the occasional leading articles. In these the message to be delivered will necessarily be distorted by passage through a foreign medium. The reviewer or leader-writer will as a rule be puzzled by, or at least out of touch with, what any book proceeding from the Catholic standpoint has to say. Direct action through the ephemeral press we cannot as yet make a principal instrument save in one particular form. That form is the subsidized weekly serious review.

Let us get the elements of this proposition clearly before us; it is a matter on which I have myself a long personal experience and to the conduct of which I can testify.

Nothing is of greater effect upon opinion—though it acts at long range and after a considerable time-lag—than a good capably-written, intelligent review of men, letters and affairs. To have its full effect it should be weekly, as I have said; a monthly review is not without effect, but not so great; a quarterly today is of hardly any effect at all, in the spread of an idea. It has sometimes a certain literary value, but little else.

Such weekly publications we are all familiar with on the anti-Catholic side, and particularly with the Radical side in politics. They almost invariably lose money. They are subsidized either by advertisement revenue or financial interests or private patrons; they could not appear without a considerable financial aid. There are indeed some weekly reviews of a very large circulation, and many of a considerable circulation, but none of them could have that circulation if they were of the standard I here presuppose. The selling price must be low, or the paper will be without effect; advertisement revenue will be small, and it is absolutely essential that the review should not be dependent upon it.

Therefore, I repeat, the venture of a high Weekly,

Catholic in tone, *must* expect a steady and regular loss. It must be published in the anticipation of such a loss, and a subsidy must be provided. That is the first necessary point; the second is that a competent Editor having been chosen, he should have a good salary with a long contract, and he should work entirely unfettered. But in choosing him there are certain points to be borne in mind and particularly that point which is my next in this catalogue: namely, that the review must deal with men and books and affairs and current politics with no more than a minimum (if even a minimum) of direct Catholic statement. Our rivals who propagate Communism or semi-Communist philosophy and who in nearly all cases are materialist and sceptical in tone, would lose their influence at once if they were to put down their doctrines in black and white and make the discussion of their theories their principal object. The cultural effect of this kind of publication is indirect. There are plenty of organs and books in which one can get direct discussion; what is needed here is the atmosphere and tone of the right side.

My third point is that the contributors must be paid on a high scale. You do not permanently get good work of a varied kind in any other fashion. Some writers will, of course, give you unpaid work, but usually on a small scale and within a narrow scope. You can trust to that sort of enthusiasm for direct action, but never for indirect.

As to the amount of subsidy required, conditions differ with every country. In England I have put it myself, in a careful study of the business and report thereon, at fifteen thousand dollars a year. The sum appears great only because men, when they talk of journalism, always think in terms of capitalism and profits, unless we are considering an organ to be used for a special purpose other than profit. Now such organs exist for the special purpose of pushing a financial policy or any other policy connected with great wealth and large expenditure. We must follow suit. Nor is the expenditure appreciable compared with that which is now to be found on all sides upon activities other than this most important and urgent one. Our missionary effort abroad, even our quasi-charitable entertainments reach a total sum of money compared with which the subsidy of a good review of this kind is insignificant: and I am convinced, both by experience and from the nature of things, that nothing can be of greater effect than a good literary paper; and that effect is unattainable without devoting to it a certain fixed annual sum.

Approach through the book is open to all of us; it is of slow effect as a rule and nearly always of indirect effect, but it is the line of least resistance. The same man who would not look at a newspaper or magazine article which seemed to him to be "sectarian" would approach with interest a book which he knew to have a special point of view, because he approaches the book in a different mood from that in which he approaches his daily paper or his magazine; a more serious mood, a more concentrated mood, and a mood prepared for the discussion and presentation of ultimate things.

There are two provinces within which the work of the book for the propagation of the Catholic culture and spirit operates; the first province is that directly concerned with a philosophy of the Faith in all its aspects. Even books of theology pure and simple have an appeal to men who know not our theology or are predisposed to hostility towards it. The presentation and discussion through the pen by a Catholic mind of general subjects— such as biography or travel—has a wider appeal. A man has but to be a Catholic and to have the Catholic culture in mind, nay, he need only be in sympathy with that culture though hardly belonging to it, to spread through whatever he writes upon the past or the present the savor of

Catholicism. He makes it known indirectly in this fashion, and this is so true that he does so even unconsciously.

Of the various forms in which this appeal through the book can work, much the most valuable is the form of history. Make men acquainted at the very root of the affair with this prime truth, that the Catholic Church made the culture which we still precariously inherit, the whole civilization in which our ancestry developed, lived fully, and wherein we partially and uncertainly live today, and that truth cannot but reflect upon the creative value of this thing which he thus newly comes across—the Catholic Church. Let a man understand that the Catholic Church made Europe and through Europe the societies which Europe has founded beyond the seas, make him understand the phrase, *"Ecclesia Mater"* in the sense of historical origins, and you have laid the foundation for all that follows.

He will in the very great majority of cases know nothing of this truth to begin with; the characters which have been presented to him as heroes of the historic past are, for the most part, characters alien to and usually hostile to Catholicism; the chief characters of Catholic source will have been presented to him as secondary or unworthy. The historians whose works he has been given as textbooks, those who inform the fiction he knows, the classics of his tongue, the body of the literature with which he is familiar, are the historians in opposition to ourselves. Write down half a dozen names: Macaulay, Carlyle, Gibbon, Mommsen, old Freeman, Motley, and the modern writer Trevelyan (this last a typical product of the highly anti-Catholic English Universities and governing class).

From Gibbon the reader learns that the discussion of those awful truths, by the definition of which our civilization was created, was the futile pastime of absurd theologians. He is also taught to believe in the same pages that the coming of the Faith destroyed the high culture of antiquity, and that we only returned to a full civic life with the disruption of Christian unity at the Renaissance and the Reformation.

Freeman tells him that his own people, the English, are the descendants of an original superior stock—by which he means the north sea pirates—and that those who are now in Europe, nations hostile to the Catholic Church, are the noble leaders of the world, are our cousins, and are almost upon the same pinnacle as ourselves. It is through such men that Prussia (generally called Germany) and England have been presented as twin stars of the first magnitude in the constellation of Europe. He is taught that our institutions (which are in truth Roman) proceed like our blood from the enemies of the ancient Græco-Roman power.

Carlyle (if we may call him an historian) put forward as his first heroic figure Frederic of Prussia; Macaulay has a hero and a villian upon whom he expends his really excellent rhetoric, and the hero is William III, a man who was in real life a pervert and a character who disgusted the mass of those who came across him; the villain is the King of France, the chief political figure of the Catholic culture in his time. Motley of course writes what is a mere panegyric of the Dutch Calvinist plutocracy in conflict with Austria and Spain. One would never guess from his pages that the power of these Dutch rebels lay in their wealth, that a good half of those whose government they took over were steadfast in the old religion, and that even now, after generations of oppression, over four out of ten among the Dutch are strongly Catholic.

Mommsen is the dull but effective, lengthy, detailed and documented attacker of our ancient culture. As for Trevelyan, he is of course nothing more than the weak echo of his greatuncle Macaulay. (I give these names only as examples, only one of them is of the first rank—Gibbon—though perhaps one may include Mommsen through his erudition, certainly not his judgment, in the same category. At any rate, the whole picture of history, the whole presentation of our development, is propaganda from the enemies' camp.)

Well, it is not difficult to rewrite history and to present historical truth. The facts are there, they have only to be presented in their due order and proportion, those which are commonly suppressed or unemphasized being given their high value, and those which have been exaggerated put in their right place. I say the task is easy save in one element: industry. The work to be undertaken is laborious, but it still lies almost untouched, though the beginnings of a reform in all this are already apparent. It should be the business of all those now entering the field of writers, even with those who do not sympathize with that by which the world may be saved, to reëstablish the truth—if only for the interest that the truth has in itself.

Remember that the effect of such writing taken up by an increasing number of men and continuously is incalculable. It comes at first in the form of a challenge; it risks violent opposition, but it has the invaluable alliance of mere fact, objective truth.

After history, fiction is, unfortunately, in our time the next department in importance. But fiction which is composed with the object of direct argument in favor of the Faith is far less effective than fiction naturally inspired by a knowledge of what the Faith is and its effects upon Society. The intermediate department of historical fiction is here particularly valuable; for the number of men and women who are affected by historical fiction when it is well and vividly written is very much greater than that of those affected by an historical narrative alone.

Then there is the department of counter-attack; the criticism and demolition of the enemy's works, the negative action of exposure not unmixed with ridicule. It is an encouragement to us in the great battle which should be before us and which is perhaps already engaged, that our opponents have already lost the framework upon which they once depended: the doctrinal framework. There are gaps in the line opposed to us; there are great voids due to this disappearance of the last vestiges of the old certitudes of anti-Catholic philosophy such as the Calvinists (that is, the Puritans) and the Rationalists had adhered to. The advance of science has not confirmed the old stark rationalism, it has on the contrary dissolved it. And the advance of documentary research and textual criticism has not confirmed the old and solid Protestant attitude towards Christian origins. It has so much undermined it that the mass of the edifice is already crumbled. It appealed in its day irrationally to the textual inspiration of the Jewish Scriptures; it proceeded by a vagary to the opposite extreme of what has been called the "higher criticism," and now this in its turn has broken down. It is our own fault if we do not occupy the works that have been abandoned.

So much for Print: that imperfect, that insufficient, but today that necessary instrument lying to our hand.

What of the second term in the proposition: a Program —a "platform"?

Here we must distinguish carefully, and the distinction we have to make may seem to some so subtle as to be difficult to grasp. There cannot be a Catholic social program, a Catholic political "platform," in the full sense of the word "Catholic." This should be a commonplace and a truism: it follows from the very nature of the Faith. The Church was not founded, has not lived, for temporal purposes; it was founded to save the souls of men. Its life is properly devoted to that object. Any social program of reform presented for the solution of temporal ills is not only subsidiary to the general task of Catholicism, but it is temporal—whereas the Faith is concerned with the eternal.

It should go without saying that an identification of the Faith with a particular scheme of social arrangements is both irrational and of evil effect. But a particular program, a particular "platform," to which men are led in a particular crisis when temporal affairs have gone awry, must necessarily arise.

Of two opposing solutions one must be more consonant with the spirit of Catholicism than the other; to meet an un-Catholic and still more an anti-Catholic solution of our present strains by mere denunciation of it, leads nowhere. When men are moved to violent indignation, indignation so violent as to lead to the extreme of civil war at the worst, and to the permanent threat of civil disorder at the best, such indignation can only be assuaged by the action of justice. The exploitation of men through the mere action of wealth, the inhuman postulates of what is called Capitalism, have led to a breakdown.

We have before us the man who says: "Rather than bear any longer the gross injustice of my condition, the cruel insecurity to which I am condemned, the arbitrary imposition by force of other men's orders for their own profit and my detriment, rather than suffer exploitation and the unbearable pressure of merely mechanical relations, I will destroy the society under which I have suffered all these things. I will at once take my revenge upon the rich to whom I am bound by no human tie of loyalty or status—since my masters have themselves denied the value of status and of the old human bonds—and I will oust them. If I must be half-a-slave for their profit I will be content to be a full slave only to the community, so

that none shall get wealthy through my labor while I
remain in despair. You tell me that in destroying property
I am destroying the family: I answer that I and my fellows
have had no property and on that account even the bond
of the family has weakened among us. We will have done
with it as the rest. We will have a new world, though it
means—and even because it means—the violent destruction of the old."

That is the spirit upon which Communism works, and
the whole present materialist revolt. The thing is at heart
an explosive uprising against injustice; even those who
lead it are some of them inspired by a flaming sense of
justice, though the greater part, the more able, and certainly the more commanding, are inspired by something
very different; being moved by hatred of all that which
made us what we are: that which made our art, and our
glory, as well as that which led us to our downfall.

Now in peril of that downfall, in peril of the loss of
that by which men should live, by which they did live (in
large degree) for centuries, by which the best instructed
of us would still desire to live, we must propose concrete
remedies. The great Encyclicals have suggested not indeed
a program, but the spirit upon which a program could be
defined.

For that program the individual proposing it must be
responsible—not the Church. Though it proceed from
individuals who are themselves Catholic or in sympathy
with Catholicism, or even from those who only perceive
(as thousands are beginning to perceive more and more
clearly) that the Faith is the one effective barrier to ruin—
yet the program is not in itself a Catholic program. It is
open to full criticism and even to denial by those who are
just as much in sympathy with Catholicism as its pro-
moters. Let them then present an alternative program,
for the program is only a means to an end; it is what we

conceive as individuals to be the product of Catholic philosophy; but its object is not to achieve itself, but a Catholic society, or at any rate to come on the way to such a society—a society in which the Catholic sense of justice shall bear fruit.

We can propose certain institutions, the resurrection of the guild, of corporate effort, of self-governing industrial bodies wherein the members shall be owners but owners shielded from the effects of unbridled competition, the extreme of which destroys the average man for the profit of the wealthy.

Collegiate property happily we already have, the Great Orders are solidly established today in a strong economic basis, let us work for their expansion and for their action not only in the educational but in the industrial field; a proposition that may seem novel but is, I think, fecund.

Let us work continually for the restoration of well divided property upon which economic freedom and therefore the dignity and permanence of the family depend. Let us propose its restoration by the working of a differential tax and its confirmation, its guarantee of endurance, by fundamental laws which control the economic pressure of great accumulations.

Above all, let us not work in blinkers with our regard confined to the palliatives of the moment. Let us not be forever concerned with amelioration of the wage system, seeing that the wage-system itself is in the very texture of the evils we propose to remedy. A living wage is an immediate and imperative necessity; things have come to such a pass that failing such regulations Society cannot continue. And the same is true of relief in every form. In so far as small property has been destroyed, men who should be owners cannot live save as wage-slaves or upon public relief. But protest in favor of sufficient wages does not get to the root of the matter. Communism gets to the root of the matter and men take to it because they clearly see that it does so. An increasingly just division and permanence of property until a determining number of the families which own shall thereby be economically free, would also go to the root of the matter, when and if it should appear as a positive political scheme which will draw men towards it, just as its immediate opponent, Communism, draws them. It is a solution which even the most desperate would understand and accept if they saw it at work.

Upon that note I close. It is a personal note, and I certainly put it forward with no other intention, nor attempt to excuse it by presenting the matter as one wherein universal agreement must be expected. Even if such a program be desirable, the pace with which it should be achieved and the methods by which it should be reached are matters for indefinitely wide debate. It is a particular proposal, and it would be both false and ridiculous to present it as a general one. But it is that which has appealed to myself in the examination of the very grave crisis upon which all this has turned, and I may add that the crisis is one which does not permit of indefinite delay.